Portfolios in the Classroom:

A Teacher's Sourcebook

ISBN 0-590-49273-X

Cover design by Vincent Ceci

Cover and interior photographs by Larry Rana

Interior illustrations by Maxie Chambliss

Book design by Ellen Matlach Hassell
for Boultinghouse & Boultinghouse, Inc.

Acknowledgments

To Carlene Payne for her encouragement
when we began sharing our knowledge
about integrated language arts and portfolios at state and national conferences.

To our students who allowed us to include
samples from their portfolios.

To the staff at Rolling Valley for their support.

Special thanks to our families for their support
and encouragement.

Portfolios in the Classroom:
A Teacher's Sourcebook

**Joan Clemmons ❖ Lois Laase
DonnaLynn Cooper ❖ Nancy Areglado
Mary Dill**

SCHOLASTIC
PROFESSIONAL **B**OOKS

New York ❖ Toronto ❖ London ❖ Auckland ❖ Sydney

Table of Contents

Introduction

In 1990, while attending the International Reading Association conference in Atlanta, Georgia, we heard many speakers discuss the use of portfolios. We learned about different styles of portfolios, but the one that interested us most engaged students in evaluating their own writing. After the conference, we decided that the staff at our school, Rolling Valley Elementary School in Springfield, Virginia, was ready to move toward portfolio assessment—a program in which students evaluate their own reading as well as their own writing.

The portfolio program we designed reflects our reading and writing classrooms and the philosophy of integrated language arts. Our school's language arts team, including grade-level representatives, the librarian, the reading specialist, and the principal, designed a portfolio implementation plan. We met and discussed the concept of using portfolios and the type of portfolio that would best show our students' growth in reading and writing. Six weeks later, teachers began implementing portfolio assessment in their classrooms.

Not every teacher jumped on the portfolio bandwagon that first year. Many teachers wanted more time to familiarize themselves with the process before implementing a portfolio program in their classrooms. Just as our reading and writing classrooms allow students time and choice to pursue interests, the faculty was given time to learn about portfolios and to choose the components that their students would include. By the beginning of the second year, all teachers were using portfolios.

As pioneers in the field of using reading and writing portfolios, we were often asked to conduct workshops throughout our school system. The second year, we began sharing our theory on using reading and writing portfolios as a method of assessment with other school districts around the country and at state and national conferences. As we reflected on our presentations, we realized that there was a tremendous need for a sourcebook on portfolios—the sourcebook we wish we had had when developing our program. It is our hope that this practical resource will help you ease your way into using portfolios as a vehicle for assessment and evaluation.

Authors examine portfolios. From left to right: Nancy, DonnaLynn, Joan, Lois, and Mary.

Joan Clemmons
  Fifth-grade teacher

Lois Laase
  Second-grade teacher

DonnaLynn Cooper
  Fourth-grade teacher

Nancy Areglado
  Reading specialist

Mary Dill
  Principal

Portfolios: Effective Assessment Tools

Why use portfolios? Alexis, a fifth grader, has an answer that says it all: *"I learned how much my thoughts grew because of using the portfolio. I wrote better stories, read more, and set goals. I became a more determined student to accomplish my goals."*

Portfolios are developmental pictures of students' progress. They allow students, parents, teachers, and administrators to understand progress in ways not possible with other types of assessment. Using portfolios as an alternative or additional means of assessment provides a way of evaluating not only the products but also the processes of learning that occur in student-centered environments. Unlike standardized tests, portfolios can showcase the processes of producing pieces of writing, such as essays, stories, and poems. Students include not only their polished pieces but their prewritings as well—brainstorming notes, mapping, webs, charts, and drafts showing revisions and rewriting.

Some of the processes of learning to read can also be shown with portfolios. A student who is in the middle of reading a book may predict and write about how he thinks the story is going to end. This piece of writing helps you understand the student's grasp of this reading skill. His writing might indicate that he is basing his prediction on a combination of what he has read so far and/or on prior knowledge—both useful tools in making predictions in reading.

Within students' portfolios you can see concepts they're learning, the thinking processes they're employing, the organization of their thoughts, and the problem-solving skills they're using. You can use this wealth of information to assess reading and writing growth across the curriculum. Just as important, portfolios empower students to be active participants in their own evaluation and learning. Students select samples of work that exemplify growth in reading and writing for inclusion in their portfolios. They are engaged in evaluating the work and in setting goals for improvement. Thus you and your students are collaborators in the assessment process.

What Is a Portfolio?

A reading and writing portfolio is a vehicle for engaging students in the process of self-evaluation and goal-setting.

A portfolio is a collection of a student's work over time that shows development in reading and writing. The contents of a portfolio focus on a student's achievements, rather than on her deficiencies. Finally, unlike a work folder in which the teacher files an assortment of graded assignments, a portfolio contains samples selected by the student.

Teachers often confuse portfolios with work folders. This chart outlines important differences:

READING/WRITING PORTFOLIOS

- Representative collection includes pivotal, improved, and best pieces.
- Samples reflect reading and writing.
- Samples show reading and writing across the curriculum.
- Collection includes samples routinely selected each grading period.
- Samples include comments by teachers and students, and indicate students' goals.

Students maintain portfolios.

WORK FOLDERS

- Samples are not chosen for specific criteria.
- Samples may or may not reflect reading and writing.
- Samples may be a collection of assorted tests.
- Samples may be collected sporadically.
- Samples usually do not include comments and goals by students.

Teachers maintain work folders.

Stacy and Danny are actively involved in assessing their work.

Students: Active in Assessment

In order for portfolios to be effective assessment tools, students must be involved in evaluating their work. In most instances, traditional assessment practices exclude students' input, with student self-evaluation and goal-setting not necessarily connected to the curriculum. In contrast, portfolio assessment includes students' input.

With your assistance, students learn how to self-evaluate and set goals for future progress. Together, you reflect on work samples, noting strengths and needs. Not only is this collaboration bound to strengthen the bonds between you and your students, it also helps students feel more involved with their own growth and more personally connected to the curriculum.

Self-evaluation and goal-setting are skills that students will use and benefit from throughout their lives. One student, Steven, reflected on the value of goal-setting:

> *"Anyone can set goals. Look at us, we are 8 and setting goals. Even when I am 65 or 85 I can set goals."*

To evaluate their own work, students need to know what makes a good piece of writing, what makes a good response to literature, and what makes a good response to knowledge acquired in content areas. One way to create this understanding is to work with students to develop and chart criteria for various types of writing samples. (*See Chapter 5, pages 44, for details.*) Using these criteria, students evaluate their strengths and set goals for improving future work. As students develop criteria for effective writing, self-evaluate their work, and set goals for improvement, they are actively participating in their own assessment and laying the foundation for more purposeful learning experiences.

The Value of Portfolios

Some of the benefits of using portfolios will be readily apparent. For example, you will probably notice early on in your portfolio program that students become more reflective about their work. However, other benefits, such as setting and working toward goals, may take some practice. The following list introduces some of the benefits of portfolio assessment. As you read on in this book, you'll learn how to achieve these benefits in your classroom.

"I have accomplished many things in reading and writing workshop. The most exciting has been trying to get my stories and poems published in a magazine." (Carrie, 5th grade)

☐ **Students retain ownership of their work; it is not just handed in to be graded by the teacher and forgotten.**

"When I evaluate a piece I see what I need to do for the next piece." (Lauren, 5th grade)

☐ **Assessment is ongoing. Students begin to apply what they learn in one piece of work to other pieces of work.**

Carly, a third-grade student, reflects on her work.

"The portfolio helps me think about what I actually learned in that paper and to remember to do certain things." (Charles, 5th grade)

☐ **Portfolios allow students to reflect on their work.**

"I will improve my spelling by using words from my own writing on my spelling list." (Aaron, 2nd grade)

☐ **When students are involved in setting goals that are important to them, they gain a sense of responsibility for their own learning. This in turn helps in creating a more student-centered curriculum.**

"I probably wouldn't have finished The Two Towers *by J.R.R. Tolkien if I had not had a goal to finish it."* (Chris, 5th grade)

☐ **Students develop increased motivation to achieve their own goals.**

"We accomplished so much when we discussed the papers in the portfolio conference. I never would have learned everything I did about Sarah and the way she learned if I had just read and graded her papers by myself." (Ms. L)

☐ **Teachers may no longer need to put a grade on every paper; instead they work with students to build a climate of trust so that they can assess work together.**

"When you read a story it gives you ideas how to write. If you are writing a story about snakes and you go and read a book about snakes, it will give you ideas about the book you are working on." (Aaron, 2nd grade)

☐ **Students apply what they are learning in reading and writing to all disciplines.**

Alison proudly shares her portfolio with her mother.

"Because I like to read mysteries I write mysteries with suspense and try to improve them by using vivid words that I found in other books."
(Amanda, 5th grade)

☐ **Students see connections between reading, writing, and thinking.**

"This piece of nonfiction about the Civil War shows I can research and write about a subject and make it sound interesting. My goal is to learn more about the Civil War. I will do that by going to the library and checking out books on the Civil War." (Karen, 5th grade)

☐ **Students and parents see that learning is a continuous process.**

"Your portfolio shows you how much you have improved. You can compare your papers and see what has improved." (Charles, 3rd grade)

☐ **Portfolios examine growth over time.**

"When I look at how I have improved it makes me feel good." (Jackie, 4th grade)

☐ **Portfolios promote self-esteem.**

"So far in my reading I have found that authors who write mysteriously and suspensefully are my favorites because their books make you think. I didn't think that at the beginning of the year. I didn't think while I read then, so I would just be reading words, but now . . . I write reading journal responses automatically when I'm excited to tell my predictions."
(Alexis, 5th grade)

☐ **Portfolios promote the value of daily reading and writing.**

"The portfolio shows the work I have been doing in reading and writing all year and shows how much I have progressed." (Jackie, 5th grade)

☐ **Portfolios support student participation and accomplishments.**

"This sample of nonfiction writing shows I can use all of the writing steps from notes to final copies and make it interesting."
(Amanda, 2nd grade)

☐ **The emphasis is not just on the final product but on the process.**

"These samples in the portfolio show so much. It is right there in black and white." (Mrs. W)

☐ **Portfolios aid in parent conferences.**

"The pictures that accompany your poetry really explain your poems well. I wish that I had put as much preparation time into what I wrote in fifth grade as you have. You are far more advanced than I was at your age." (Mrs. H)

☐ **Portfolios help parents get involved in their child's work.**

"It just wouldn't show a grade. It would show the work you've been doing also."
(Mark, 5th grade)

"On the report card, the grades themselves tell me only how my son is doing compared to everyone else. The samples in the portfolio, on the other hand, reveal much about my child. I am thrilled with what I see here." (Mrs. W)

☐ **Portfolios compliment report cards.**

School-Based Research Supports Portfolios

Teachers at Rolling Valley Elementary School, an ethnically diverse school in Springfield, Virginia, have been using portfolios since 1991. The following results of a study during the first two years show the ongoing benefits of portfolio assessment.

FIRST YEAR:

243 students responded to a questionnaire regarding their use of portfolios.

- 92 percent felt that using the portfolios helped them show their parents more than the report card showed.
- 86 percent felt that the portfolios made it easier for them to tell their parents how well they were doing in school.
- 88 percent said they are better able to set goals for themselves since using portfolios.

SECOND YEAR:

344 students completed the same questionnaire that had been used the previous year. More students responded, however, results were almost identical.

- 93 percent felt that using the portfolios helped them show their parents more than the report cards showed.
- 85 percent felt that the portfolios made it easier for them to tell their parents how well they were doing in school.
- 89 percent said they are better able to set goals since using portfolios.

What Teachers Say

After using portfolios for two years, teachers at Rolling Valley Elementary School reflected on the use of this assessment tool in their classrooms. They felt strongly that portfolios helped them examine their students' growth over time—comparing students' earliest samples with quarterly samples gave them a clear picture of this growth. Portfolios also helped the teachers assess their students more thoroughly than in the past. By developing criteria for effective writing *with* their students, teachers felt that both they and their students were looking for the same thing when assessing a piece of writing. Teachers also commented on their students' feelings of accomplishment, especially at the end of each year when they looked back on earlier samples and could see their progress.

The experience of Rolling Valley's teachers validates research on how portfolios help teachers. "Research studies and anecdotal data from portfolio projects suggest that teachers perceive the process of portfolio assessment as a worthwhile experience—they pay more attention to students; learn more about students' needs; are able to discern growth; and learn more about how assessment, instruction, and student performance fit together." ("Portfolios: Panacea or Pandora's Box?" by Sheila Valencia, *Educational Performance Assessment*; Riverside Publishing Co., 1991)

Portfolios: A Natural Outgrowth of Reading and Writing Classrooms

Think about what goes on in your classroom. Do your students read and write daily? Are they allowed to choose what they read and what they write? Is language arts integrated across your curriculum? Do you find yourself teaching mini-lessons to address students' needs as they arise? Do you read to your students? If you answered *yes* to these questions, chances are you've got a reading and writing classroom, and the foundation you need to implement portfolio assessment in your classroom.

In reading and writing classrooms, teachers create atmospheres that encourage students to be actively involved in their own learning. Throughout the day, they're engaged in meaningful activities and immersed in reading, writing, speaking, and listening. In short, they're involved in processes that allow them to discover new ideas, to think critically, and to gain knowledge.

Portfolios are a natural outgrowth of these classrooms. To understand the instrumental role that portfolios can play in this setting, it's helpful to take a closer look at the distinguishing characteristics of reading and writing classrooms.

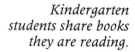

Kindergarten students share books they are reading.

Students and teachers are a community of learners.

The climate of a reading and writing classroom is integrally linked to students being encouraged to function as a community of learners. The atmosphere is one of acceptance—students are risk-takers, ideas are shared by both students and teacher, and opinions are valued. In this cooperative environment, students learn from students, students learn from the teacher, and the teacher learns from the students. Students accept responsibility for their learning and contribute as members of a community of learners.

Flexible groups abound.

In a reading and writing classroom, the size and composition of groups vary according to the purpose of the activity. Heterogeneous, homogeneous, cooperative, collaborative, and whole class groupings, as well as partnerships and individual student units, are all possibilities. For example, you might group students by twos for sharing and editing pieces of writing or gather small groups together to work on specific needs, such as expanding sentences or improving word attack skills.

The basic ingredients of flexible groups are: 1) they are determined by student needs, and 2) they are short-lived. Flexible groupings enhance students' self-concept because they work with other students regardless of ability. Flexible groups motivate achievement by giving all students a chance to contribute, by addressing special needs, and by capitalizing on students' areas of expertise.

Mini-lessons teach skills and strategies.

Brief demonstration lessons are presented to large or small groups of students with similar needs. Mini-lesson teaching materials include children's literature, the teacher's own writing, and students' writings.

❖ SAMPLE MINI-LESSON 1 ❖

Using Dialogue

If several students want to use dialogue in their writing, teach a mini-lesson on the skill using trade books with good examples of dialogue as instructional materials. Instead of reading rules from a textbook, have students investigate text samples to see where the author uses quotation marks, commas, end-of-sentence marks, and paragraphs. Encourage students to develop their own rules based on their investigations. To facilitate instruction, make overhead transparencies of pages that include dialogue.

❖ SAMPLE MINI-LESSON 2 ❖

Responding to Concepts Learned in Content Areas

Before asking students to respond to a concept covered in a content area, present a mini-lesson on ways to write a response. Use examples of well-written responses from previous classes or teacher-made samples as instructional materials. Ask students to discuss the criteria that make these good responses. Use these discussions to help students learn how to plan their own answers, write in complete sentences, stick to the topic, use correct terminology, include drawings to clarify points, and so on.

Alina and Tammy brainstorm criteria for writing responses.

Language arts is integrated across the curriculum.

There are many advantages to integrating language arts across the curriculum. Integrating language arts gives teachers more time to teach. Rather than set aside a separate time for teaching reading and writing, these areas can easily be included in all subject areas throughout the day. For example, if students are studying plant life, you could introduce trade books about plants. You could also read and write poetry about plant life. When students write about what they are learning in all subject areas, they tend to remember the material more accurately. Writing about a topic or concept in their own words gives students one more opportunity to process the material. Combining reading and writing with other subject areas encourages students to make connections between ideas and to see relationships.

Eight-year-old Stuart demonstrates how language arts is integrated across the curriculum in a reading and writing classroom in his response to *In Coal Country* by Judith Hendershot (Knopf, 1987), a story about growing up in a coal-mining town. Not only had Stuart read the book prior to writing his response, he also participated in a social studies group discussion of life in a coal-mining town. In language arts lessons he learned about the use of flashbacks as a literary technique. Stuart used this prior knowledge to personalize his reading of the story by putting himself back into that period of time:

> Stuart
>
> In Coal Country
>
> It's hard to remember back to those hard working days of 1912 when our father worked in the coal mine 12 hours every night. Each morning our mother would send us to get dad. I would always ask him do you have any cookies left? I would look in his blue and white lunch pail. He didn't. There would just be a rotten apple and a half eaten ham sandwich. Then I would walk with him to the gas station to get flour. Mr. Flibs would always give us an Eskimo Pie and a lemon candy stick. Dad would buy tobacco for his pipe. I said isn't there enough smoke around here?

Teachers read to students daily.

In reading and writing classrooms, teachers read to students daily. This is an opportunity to familiarize students with both nonfiction and fiction. Reading to students daily also motivates and heightens their interest in reading. They become familiar with new authors and new pieces of literature. Read-alouds build language and background knowledge, as well as extending students' vocabulary. In addition to promoting reading, you can use the read-alouds to model reading and writing strategies.

Three of the many sources you might want to consult in selecting books for read alouds are:

📖 *The New Read-Aloud Handbook* by Jim Trelease (Penguin, 1989),

📖 *Using Picture Storybooks to Teach Literary Devices* by Susan Hall (The Oryx Press, 1990), and

📖 *Eyeopeners!* by Beverly Kobrin (Penguin, 1988).

Emily and Melissa select books for reading.

Students are given time to read daily.

Students in reading and writing classrooms read quality children's literature every day. Students might select books related to a unit of study, books by one author, or books in a particular genre such as historical fiction. School librarians and media specialists are wonderful resources for helping students choose books to read.

This time to read, sometimes known as SSR (sustained silent reading) or DEAR (drop everything and read), is a vital ingredient in the program. When students have time to read daily, their reading ability increases dramatically. Reading daily also gives students opportunities to practice self-monitoring strategies that aid in comprehension: assessing what they know and don't know, connecting new knowledge with past experiences, rereading texts, and personalizing reading to construct meaning.

Students are given choice in what they read.

Although general curriculum topics are often determined by the school or teacher, students are given choice in reading materials and are encouraged to read a wide range of literature genres. Students might read stories in basal or literature series but more often will choose trade books from classroom collections.

📖 Kindergarten and lower-primary classrooms may have on hand highly predictable literature, or books that have rhyme, rhythm, or repetition, to aid emergent readers. Bill Martin's classic *Brown Bear, Brown Bear, What Do You See?* (Holt, 1970) is an example of a predictable book that also makes sense.

Jared shares an interesting part of his book with Jeffrey.

Trade books that relate to content areas are important classroom additions. For example, Cynthia Rylant's Caldecott winner, *When I Was Young in the Mountains* (Dutton, 1982), supports a study of communities. Students learning division might like to read Pat Hutchin's *The Doorbell Rang* (Greenwillow, 1986). Reference books such as *Books Kids Will Sit Still For* by Judy Freeman (Bowker, 1990) and *Best Books for Children* edited by John Gillespie and Corrine Naden (Bowker, 1990) are useful in identifying titles that tie in with particular topics.

Students may read many books written by the same author. By reading the books themselves or listening to you read, students learn about the author's writing style. For example, you can immerse your students in literature by Mary Downing Hahn. As you and your students read the different mysteries written by this author, such as *Following the Mystery Man* (Clarion, 1988), you can share and discuss the different passages found in her books.

Students read a variety of genres. Incorporating books from multiple genres, such as biographies and mysteries, helps students become more sophisticated readers and writers. Check out books from the school's reading center and from school and public libraries to help build a rich collection in your classroom.

Trade books that combine fiction with nonfiction are particularly popular with students. Joanna Cole's *Magic School Bus at the Waterworks* (Scholastic, 1986) is an example of such a book. Factual information about the difficult concept of the water cycle is presented in an imaginative and amusing fictional field trip to a reservoir system.

As students discuss and share books with each other during book talks, they are introducing new literature to their peers who are then often motivated to read those books. Exploring books connected with themes or units of study exposes children to creative and different ways that themes can be developed. It *is* true that students learn to read by reading.

Students and teachers reflect on their learning.

In reading and writing classrooms, students reflect on what they read through a variety of response forms, such as reading journal entries, drama, literature discussions, and visual arts. Responding to literature in different ways enhances students' understandings of what they read. For example, reading journals help students connect their thoughts on pieces of literature by responding in writing. When students work in cooperative groups to write and present skits, plays, and puppet shows based on literature, they are actively engaged in creative thinking, problem solving, and risk taking. Students also respond to literature they read in small heterogeneous group discussions and by creating and sharing projects based on books they read. When children have opportunities to express their understandings of literature in various ways, they move beyond simple retellings and develop higher-order thinking and language skills.

Amanda's thoughtful response to *Hansi* by Maria Hirschmann (Tindale, 1974) demonstrates this. In a letter to her friend Karen, Amanda not only relates to the main character in *Hansi* but also connects new information from the story to her own familiar experiences. She continues to interact with the story as she describes her own feelings and thoughts:

> May 26, 1992
>
> Dear Karen,
> I have just finish reading the book Hansi by M. Hirschmann.
> I can't believe it took me so long to figure out that this book was an autobiography. I guess it took me such a long time because of all the hardships that had been through. It never dawned on me before that people actually lived through the things that she did. I am also very happy that her life is finally started to get better, and she is finally content.
> Your friend,
> Amanda
>
> Dear Amanda,
> I would have never guessed the anyone could go through things like that. This was a great responce! Karon H.

Students are given time to write daily.

In reading and writing classrooms, students have daily opportunities to write—to use what they are learning about the language of print to communicate with others. Writing daily during a regularly scheduled block of time helps students grow as writers. In your reading and writing classrooms, allow time for students to use the steps of the writing process—prewriting, drafting, revising, editing, and sharing—and model those steps when possible.

Students need time to brainstorm and organize their ideas before drafting. If they choose to write about unfamiliar topics, they need time to research, read, and gather information. After drafting, students revise, confer with you and other students, and revise and edit again. Finally, they share or publish their writings.

Students' writing styles, skills, and strategies may suggest opportunities for modeling and mini-lessons. Students can then practice newly acquired skills and experiment with a variety of writing styles daily. The classroom is a writer's workshop in which students are risk-takers whose efforts are valued and respected by all members.

Students are given choice in what they write.

Students in reading and writing classrooms are encouraged to write for different purposes and to consider their audiences when planning their pieces. Seldom is the entire class given the same title or prompt, such as a story starter or a picture, which often results in students producing very similar pieces. Instead, students might select ideas from a list of possible writing topics they brainstormed earlier in the year. Students can keep copies of this list in their writing folders and add their own ideas throughout the year.

Students' writings, both expository and narrative, can take different forms. They might model their writings after particular literature they have read and enjoyed: for example, while studying point of view, one student read *The True Story of the Three Little Pigs* by Jon Scieszka (Penguin, 1989). This inspired her to write a version of *Little Red Riding Hood* from the wolf's point of view.

Students can also respond to material they learn in content areas by writing poems, plays, descriptions, and explanations. Fifth-grade students Lindsay and Kathryn collaborated on the following poem after studying the American Revolution.

THE REVOLUTION

If I were to be a woman soldier,
I'd carry a gun upon my shoulder.
Upon instruction I would fire
At the British who would soon retire.

I'd like to ride along with Paul
    Revere,
Through the mysterious woods I
    would peer.
Knocking and pounding on all the
    doors,
To tell the people British wanted war!

A soldier fired but no one knew,
Which side it came from, out of the
    blue,
From that shot on, both sides fired,
And all the soldiers grew very tired.

Well the British lost oh my oh well.
Americans were very proud to tell
That they had won the Revolution
And so they came to one solution.

The Americans weren't at all greedy,
As a result they signed a peace
    treaty.
So from now on they would fight no
    more,
Because the peace treaty ended the
    war.

Lindsay and Kathryn, 5th grade

It would be difficult for standardized tests or report cards to show the processes of learning that Lindsay and Kathryn used to produce their final product. They read literature about the Revolutionary War and read poems to understand the elements of poetry. They brainstormed ideas for their poem and worked together writing drafts. They used dictionaries and other references as they revised and edited. They shared their poem with peers for reactions and comments before typing it on the computer for publication.

This process—prewriting, drafting, revising, sharing—can be exhibited in a portfolio. When students select their topics and their styles of writing, and are encouraged to revise their work, they are becoming writers. Through experimentation and daily practice they become skilled writers, who are proud of their work.

Katie and Laura write in their journals.

Steven confers with Mrs. Clemmons about his writing.

Large blocks of time are available for reading and writing.

Time is as important as choice in reading and writing classrooms. When students are given choice in what they read and write, they must also be given time to pursue their choices, to become actively involved with language, and to become effective readers and writers. During these large blocks of time, you can help students become involved with language by:

❖ conducting mini-lessons on reading and writing strategies,

❖ providing time for quiet reading and writing,

❖ working with individuals and small groups as necessary,

❖ reading aloud to students, and

❖ setting aside time for sharing.

Assessment is collaborative and ongoing.

Tests that measure acquisition of basic skills are not authentic assessments of literacy achievement in reading and writing classrooms. Instead, assessment must reflect the philosophy and goals of developing avid readers and writers who are skilled with communication processes. That is, can students listen, speak, read, and write, and can they use these processes to gain knowledge as well as to provide pleasure? The assessment program needs to be continuous, evaluating not only the products but also the processes of reading and writing activities.

In addition, if students are expected to become independent learners, they must become active participants in their own evaluation; in other words, you and your students collaborate in the process of evaluation. Together, you develop criteria to evaluate reading and writing. Through teacher modeling and practice, students

Karen pulls her portfolio to review her goals.

learn how to evaluate their own work. They look at their needs to set goals for future attainment. When you continually assess students by observing and by gathering information, including the goals students set, you can more precisely group students according to their needs and more effectively determine your instructional program. Portfolios are a way to address this assessment need in reading and writing classrooms. They are a way of documenting student work over time for collaborative and ongoing reflection, evaluation, goal-setting, and instructional planning.

What the Research Says

"Portfolios are likely to be a far richer source of information about a student's literacy achievement, progress, and ongoing development than other, more formal sources. Besides, portfolios have the potential to contribute to everybody's understanding of the student's ongoing learning in ways which are positive and grounded in reality."

Portfolio Assessment in the Reading-Writing Classroom by R. Tierney, M. Carter, L. Desai (Christopher-Gordon, 1991)

Implementing a Portfolio Program: A Plan for School, Teacher, and Parent Involvement

Once you've made a commitment to reading and writing classrooms, portfolios will be a natural choice for assessing student progress. As you begin, it's helpful to keep in mind that the process of developing, implementing, and maintaining an effective portfolio program takes time and careful planning. You'll need to think about such tasks as introducing staff, students, and parents to portfolios; developing guidelines; and selecting components before you begin implementation.

Following is an outline for implementing portfolio assessment school-wide. It is similar to the two-year plan that Rolling Valley Elementary School used. There, a team of teachers, specialists, and an administrator worked together to develop and implement their plan. You might want to consider forming a similar team in your own school to coordinate the portfolio process. However, if you're implementing portfolios as an individual teacher, a modified plan is included here. Finally, for both schoolwide and single-classroom implementation, this chapter concludes with detailed suggestions for bringing parents on board.

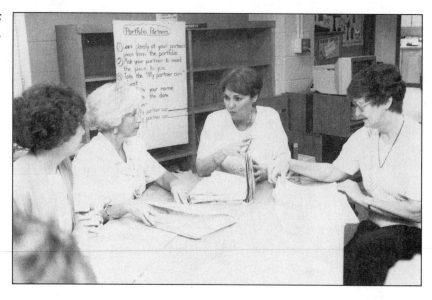

Teachers develop portfolio guidelines in a grade-level workshop.

Schoolwide Implementation: Year One

1. Introduce the concept of portfolio assessment to faculty at a schoolwide meeting. (If your school administrators are not already involved, invite them!)

2. Help staff members gain a better understanding of portfolio assessment by regularly sharing articles and other references that support the use of this alternative method of assessment.

3. Attend sessions on portfolio assessment at language arts conferences and after-school workshops to learn more.

4. Form a team of teachers and language arts specialists to develop guidelines for selecting portfolio components. (*See Chapter 4, pages 35–42, for details on selecting components.*) Individual teachers can refer to these guidelines to select the components that best support their classroom needs.

5. Conduct grade-level workshops to explain portfolio guidelines and answer teachers' questions, as well as to document teachers' suggestions. (Teachers at Rolling Valley had input in all stages of implementation.)

6. Introduce the concept of portfolio assessment to the school community, particularly to parents. Report on the implementation process in your school newsletter; share information at back-to-school night, PTA meetings, and parent-teacher conferences.

7. Introduce students to portfolio assessment. You might, for example, invite local artists to display and discuss their professional portfolios.

8. Begin implementation. At Rolling Valley, some teachers began implementation immediately while others felt more comfortable waiting until later in the year. (*See Chapter 6, pages 53–60, for step-by-step guidelines on what to do each quarter—from gathering supplies to sending portfolio samples to students' next teachers.*)

9. Organize a volunteer parent group to assist teachers with their portfolio workload on a weekly basis. For example, parents can assist with audiotaping reading samples and videotaping student performances and projects. (*See page 95 for reproducible parent volunteer letter.*)

10. Invite the school's reading specialist to model lessons on using portfolios in the classroom.

11. Form a collaborative support group and meet regularly throughout the year. Bring actual portfolios. Share successes, problems, and suggestions.

12. Decide how and when you will share portfolios with parents. (Teachers at Rolling Valley agreed to send portfolios home four times a year with report cards. After review, parents return the portfolios to school.)

13. Offer in-service training sessions and workshops on portfolio assessment throughout the year. For example, invite teachers who attend portfolio sessions at conferences to share information with colleagues.

14. Find out about electronic portfolio assessment software (such as the *Grady Profile*, Aurbach and Associates). Obtain a demo program and hold sessions to inform and train teachers.

Schoolwide Implementation: Year Two and Beyond

By year two, all teachers at Rolling Valley were using portfolios in their classrooms. While the basic plan doesn't change from year one to year two and beyond, what can change is the number of components you are using. If you're just getting started in portfolio assessment, you may feel more comfortable focusing on one or two components in year one. In year two, strive to include more components. Remember, the more components you select to include, the more comprehensive the developmental picture of the child becomes.

Rolling Valley teachers plan strategies for the continuing use of portfolios.

Adapting the Plan for Individual Teachers

Although the collegiality of whole-school involvement is certainly a big plus, individual teachers can adapt the school plan as described in this chapter. Even if a teacher is the sole enthusiast for portfolio assessment in the school building or school system, single classroom implementation can still have profound benefits. Although the following suggestions are designed for teachers who will initiate a portfolio program at the beginning of the school year, you can implement portfolio assessment at any time of the school year.

1. Identify components to be included in student portfolios that best meet your students' needs and the objectives of your classroom and the school. The number of components should be sufficient to show students' development in reading and writing. (*See Chapter 4, page 35–42, for more information.*)

2. Educate and inform parents about your classroom portfolio program. Discuss portfolios at back-to-school night and in class newsletters.

3. Invite parents to assist with the program. (*See sample page 95 for parent volunteer letter.*)

4. Use portfolios when conferring with parents. Send portfolios home several times a year with instructions for parents to return them to school, the exception being at the end of the year when students keep them.

5. Attempt to interest a colleague in beginning a portfolio program.

6. Increase interest and use of portfolios in your school by sharing successes on a regular basis with other colleagues. Offer to present workshops on portfolios. Invite students to present with you.

7. Continue to learn more about portfolios as an assessment tool. Attend conferences sponsored by your state reading association and/or its local chapter.

8. Inquire about teacher support groups in your area. Join a local group and form a portfolio support group within the larger group.

Teacher support group meets to share ideas.

Mrs. Clemmons shares a portfolio with an excited parent.

A Plan for Involving Parents

Just as parents treasure baby books that record early memories of their child's development, so will they treasure portfolios, records of grade-level landmarks. Portfolios give parents an opportunity to see, from one quarter to the next, what their child has accomplished and what he wants to achieve. Of course, the more children and parents interact together with portfolios, the stronger the home/school connection will be.

Helping parents understand portfolio assessment is a continuous process. Following are seven ways you can keep your students' parents informed. Samples of letters and forms for parents appear in the appendix at the end of this book. You may reproduce them as is or adapt them to meet your own needs.

1. Introductory Letter

Introduce your portfolio program with a letter or memo to parents that briefly explains this assessment technique. Send a copy of this letter home with each student or include it in an issue of a schoolwide newsletter. (*See page 95 for a sample introductory letter.*)

2. Back-to-School Night

Back-to-school night is another opportunity to explain the portfolio program. Invite your school administrator to show support by discussing advantages of using reading and writing portfolios for assessment and evaluation. Individual teachers can discuss the components that will be included in their portfolios. Demonstrate how students will evaluate the work they select for their portfolios. (*See Chapter 5, page 43–50, for suggestions on teaching self-evaluation and goal-setting.*)

3. Parent/Teacher Conferences

Parent/teacher conferences are excellent occasions for sharing students' portfolios in conjunction with other assessment tools, such as report cards. Take time to explain or review the portfolio program, including the student-evaluation process. Help parents see their child's growth by comparing baseline samples, those taken at the beginning of the school year, with quarterly samples. Refer parents to written student evaluations and teacher comments that highlight strengths of each portfolio sample. Look at the child's stated goals to help parents see the child's targeted areas of improvement. Reinforce that the portfolio compliments the report card by showing what the child has accomplished in reading and writing.

Dear Stephen,

I'm glad I kept your portfolio an extra day so that I didn't have to rush through your work. Reading J. R. R. Tolkein's books has helped you appreciate good literature. When I first read these books I loved them, too. I was caught up in the excitement of the adventure and the unfolding story, but I didn't learn as much as you are learning. You are learning how to interact with the story in a very personal way through your reading responses and your book talks. You are asking questions and making predictions. You are appreciating the power of well-chosen words to describe various settings, to develop characters, and to depict intense emotions. I see growth in your ability to express your ideas verbally and in writing. Thanks for sharing your work with me. I'm proud of you!

Love,
Mom

A parent's response to her son's portfolio.

4. Explanatory Letter to Accompany the Portfolio

One way to help parents get a clear picture of a portfolio is to write a letter explaining the portfolio's contents. Focus on helping parents understand what is in the portfolio and what the contents represent. Enclose a copy of the letter in each student's portfolio. (*See pages 96–97 for sample explanatory letters to parents.*)

5. Letters from Parents to Their Children

Invite parents to respond to their child's portfolio in letter forms. This not only encourages parents to read and study the contents more carefully, but the positive comments they write will boost their child's self-esteem. These letters are also another means of communication between parent and child. Provide paper for parents' responses to facilitate participation. Include these letters in children's portfolios. (*See page 98 for sample of an invitation to parents.*)

Mrs. Hoyle, a parent volunteer, assists a teacher.

6. Parent Questionnaires

A series of questionnaires is one way to gather feedback from parents on the effectiveness of portfolios. Following are results of four informal questionnaires teachers at Rolling Valley sent home with portfolios:

- 95 percent of 60 parents returning questionnaire #1 were in favor of portfolios.

- 93 percent of 100 parents returning questionnaire #2 indicated a positive response to portfolios.

- 97 percent of 120 parents returning questionnaire #3 made positive comments and indicated that they had a better understanding of their child's development in reading and writing.

- 98 percent of 102 parents returning questionnaire #4 were in favor of using portfolios.

"It's interesting to see how Susan makes choices as to which sample of work to select, and how she is progressing in her self-evaluation."

"Our child's portfolio lets us understand the grades in the same way the teacher sees them."

"By looking at the samples, I can see the areas where my child needs special attention."

It's always encouraging to get such positive responses. But the questionnaires can also help you become aware of and address parents' concerns. For example,

parents might wonder if using portfolios takes time away from teaching. You might address this concern in a phone call or in an explanatory letter to all parents to help them understand that using portfolios is part of the way your students are learning. Be sure to share results of questionnaires with parents, teachers, and administrators. (*See pages 91–101 for three sample questionnaires.*)

7. Parent Volunteer Program

Asking parents to assist in implementing portfolio assessment is a sure way to encourage understanding of the assessment tool. Request volunteers through the school newsletter and at back-to-school night, or send sign-up forms home with students. Parents can help at school on a regular basis or may be called as needed. Some of the tasks you might ask parents to help with include:

- ❖ assisting younger students in reading or retelling stories on audiotape;

- ❖ photocopying text samples and other samples or forms as necessary;

- ❖ videotaping students;

- ❖ performing clerical duties such as writing students' names on folders, audiotape packets, envelopes, and so on.

(*See page 95 for sample parent volunteer letter.*)

Components of a Portfolio

The components of a reading and writing portfolio present a picture of a child's progress. In a reading and writing classroom where students have choice in what they read and write and where they have time to read and write every day, these components will naturally evolve. When you select components to include in your students' portfolios, consider both the classroom and the school instructional program. Ask yourself how each component highlights a different aspect of a student's reading and writing development.

Because reading and writing classrooms integrate language arts across the curriculum, the components you select will also reflect reading and writing in the various subject areas, including mathematics, science, health, and social studies. Of course, including a variety of different components affords you a more complete picture of each student's development. Detailed descriptions of nine components follow.

*Students discuss a
reading-journal entry.*

1. Baseline Samples

Baseline samples are students' first portfolio pieces. They are a student's earliest samples of work representing each of the components you select, for example, reading-journal entries, learning-log entries, and first pieces of writing. The first audio tapes and video tapes students make can also serve as baseline samples. Baseline samples are compared to others collected throughout the year to assess growth and achievement in reading and writing. These samples are also useful in tailoring lessons to meet the needs of your students.

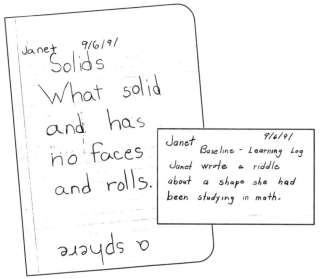

Janet 9/6/91
Solids
What solid
and has
no faces
and rolls.

Janet   9/6/91
Baseline - Learning Log
Janet wrote a riddle
about a shape she had
been studying in math.

a sphere

Learning-log baseline sample

2. Reading-Journal Entries

A reading journal is a notebook in which the student responds to literature. Reading journals are also known as literature response journals, literary journals, and reading logs. Students can also record the same kinds of responses in a dialogue journal in which the teacher or another student writes back or responds to what the student writes about the literature.

Reading journals encourage students to go beyond just writing simple summaries of what they read. Students can explain how they relate to characters or to what they read. They can make comparisons and predictions, give opinions about the literature and the author, discuss an author's writing style, generate new interpretations or points of view, answer open-ended questions, and respond personally to what they read.

Responding to literature in a variety of ways encourages students to think critically about what they read, to construct meaning from the literature, and to connect writing and reading. For you, reading journals are an important way of evaluating students' understandings of what they read.

> June 1, 1992
>
> Dear Alexis,
> I have recently finished reading the book
> _Shades of Gray_ by C. Reeder.
> The main character is a boy named Will
> who eventually becomes a dynamic character.
> The thing that interested me most that Will
> changed the same way that Hansi did in the
> book Hansi. In _Shades of Gray_, Will goes to
> live with uncle who didn't fight in the Civil
> War because it was against his beliefs. At first
> Will thinks uncle was a wimp and not a real
> man, but soon begins to realize that it doesn't
> matter what other people think or do, but what
> matters is to do what you think is right and
> follow what you believe in.
> In _Hansi_, she learns that it is important to
> forgive people, and even if they betray you one thousand
> times, one thousand times you should forgive them.
> I thoroughly enjoyed both of these books and I
> think that both of these lessons are important and
> I wish that someday everyone could learn them.
>
> Your friend,
> K.R.
>
> Dear A.R.,
> I read this book too. If there was a war
> going on, do you think you would fight just to
> help slave owners keep their slaves? No, well
> at least I wouldn't. Will is right, it doesn't matter what other people
> think or do. Yes it is important to learn these lessons. I agree you
> should learn them well. I wouldn't fight either.
> Alexis

If you choose reading journals as a portfolio component, have each student select a sample to include in the portfolios each quarter. To facilitate the selection process, and to make sure students have an opportunity to reflect on their responses before choosing one, have the students keep their written responses to literature together in a composition book.

3. Learning-Log Entries

Students use learning logs to record responses to topics of study in various content areas such as social studies, science, health, and mathematics. You might ask students to write in the log at various times during a lesson: at the beginning of a lesson—to activate prior knowledge of the subject, during a lesson as an independent activity, and at the end of a lesson for closure or for helping to evaluate and plan for the next lesson. For example, before beginning a math lesson on division, you might ask students to write what they know about division. In the middle of the lesson, students might respond to the question, "What is one step in division that is causing you trouble?" At the end of the lesson, students can explain in their own words how to divide.

This type of writing gives students opportunities to interact with content material and encourages them to think about what they are learning in any subject area. Try to give students time to write in their learning logs at least every few days. For learning logs to be most effective, you'll need to respond verbally or in writing to students' entries.

Again, if you choose learning logs as one of your portfolio components, have students add an entry to their portfolios each quarter. As with reading journals, it's important that students have a notebook to keep all their responses together. This makes it easier for students to see ongoing progress and facilitates selecting sample responses for the portfolios.

Learning-log entry—a response to the study of the heart

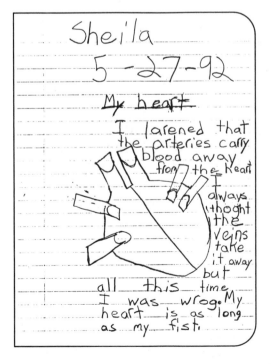

> Sheila
> 5-27-92
> My heart
> I larened that the arteries carry blood away from the heart. I always thought the veins take it away but all this time, I was wrog. My heart is as long as my fist.

A third-grade student reads her published piece.

4. Writing Samples

A writing sample is an original piece of writing, fiction or nonfiction, that shows the writing process. The sample is usually a draft, unless the entry is a published piece that represents all the steps of the writing process. In reading and writing classrooms, students write daily and have a choice in what they write. In addition, they write in a variety of genres and for different audiences. These students begin to identify themselves as authors who write for different purposes. They can reflect this variety in the selections they choose to include in their portfolios.

Ask each student to choose an improved or best piece of writing for her portfolio. At least twice a year have students include writing samples that illustrate the steps in the writing process, including prewriting, drafting, revising, editing, and sharing. By including writing samples from different times of the year, children can see how their editing and revising skills are developing. They also learn that the emphasis is not only on the final product but on process and growth as well. Of course, viewing a piece from the beginning of the process offers you, the teacher, valuable assessment information.

Writing folders are a good way to help students organize their writing samples. When it's time to select samples or assemble drafts representing different steps in the writing process, all of a student's work will be in one place.

Karen's web and final persuasive paragraph on drugs

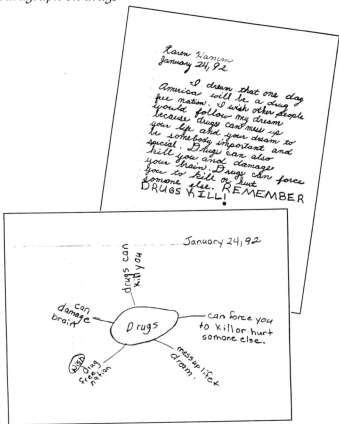

Record of books taped and student self-evaluation of a book talk

Date	Tape #	Title	Danny	Author
9/11/91	0 /25	The Big Green Thing		M. Schlein
9/8/92	96 /72	Space Rock		
3/30/92	73 /130	Sharks		A. McGovern

Karen Hansen   March 20, 92
    This tape shows that I can plan a 3 to 5 minute response. It also shows I can talk orally to a group of people.
    Goals: My goal is to not say well ah um so many times in my talk

5. Audiotape Recordings

Students use audiocassettes to record themselves reading aloud, retelling stories, or presenting book talks. These recordings are a way of evaluating a student's development of oral language and sentence structure. By listening to the oral fluency, the student's decoding ability can also be noted. Tapes that include a student's discussion of a story can help you measure comprehension. Students might read aloud a passage from a favorite book or try any of the following variations.

❖ Emergent readers may be most comfortable retelling familiar stories, such as *The Three Little Pigs,* for their audiotape component. In addition to retelling stories on tape, students might record verbal responses to questions about the stories.

❖ Students who choose to record themselves reading stories aloud might also record their thoughts about the stories or illustrations.

❖ Students can read aloud their own writings.

❖ Experienced readers might record a book talk or reading conference in which they read aloud short selections; give brief story summaries; discuss character development, setting, theme, and favorite passages; share personal responses; and invite questions and comments from classmates. Record the entire conference.

If audio tapes will be part of your portfolios, have each student choose a piece of literature to retell, read aloud, and/or discuss in a reading conference each grading period. You might suggest that students write and include evaluations of their tape recordings. (*See page 109 for a guide to audiotape recordings.*)

Jason tape records a book he wrote.

6. Videotape Recordings

Videotapes offer a unique way of looking at students in a reading and writing classroom. They provide you and your students with a way to observe reading, speaking, and listening skills. You might, for example, videotape students performing original plays, sharing projects, or reading aloud to a group of students. Details on each of these follow.

❖ **Dramatizations:** Videotaping students' dramatizations helps the students get a sense of their oral language development. You and the students can also observe how they use eye contact, voice intonation, and body language to convey meaning. When students write the scripts for these dramatizations, you can also record and observe creativity and writing skills at work. Finally, videotaping a performance lets you assess students' abilities to work with others to produce a play.

❖ **Project Presentations:** Videotapes are a way of including three-dimensional projects in portfolios. In addition to recording both the project itself and the student's explanation, videotapes capture a student's public-speaking ability, organization skills (in speech and in presentation), creativity, and ability to explain and answer questions about a project. You might, for example, videotape a group of students sharing a report on communities that includes designing and building a house.

❖ **Read Alouds:** Videotapes of students reading books to an audience or retelling a story allow you to observe expression, fluency, word attack skills, and voice projection. You can also capture students' interaction with their audiences.

Encourage students to view their performances as soon after the taping as possible, and to invite peers to the review for helpful feedback. After viewing, ask students to discuss strengths and possibilities for improvement. Have students use the criteria for public speaking as they write evaluations of their performances and set goals for improving future presentations. (*See page 116 for sample criteria chart for public speaking.*)

Students help a peer evaluate a videotape recording.

Reading Log

Date	Title	Author	Genre	Rate	Pages	
9/9/91	The Great Flood	E. and M. Hubge	Non-fiction	5	110	1
9/10/91	STARS	Seymour Simon	Non-fiction	1	50	2
9/26/91	Howliday Inn	James Howe	fiction	3	195	3
10/4/91	Magic in the Park	Ruth Chew	fiction	4	181	4
						5
10/29/91	Jupiter	Seymour Simon	Nonfiction	1	50	6
10/29/91	Saturn	Seymour Simon	nonfiction	1	50	7
10/2/91	The Finding	Nina Bawden	fiction	6	47	8
10/29/91	Boy	Roald Dahl	Biography	4	298	9
/91	Matilda	Roald Dahl	fiction	5	320	10
		Second Quarter				
11/../91	More about Paddington	Michael Bond	fiction	3	127	11
11/1/91	Homer Price	Robert McCloskey	fiction	2	204	12
11/../91	Dracula's Castle	Vic Crume	fiction	1	100	13
1/3/91	Tasmania	Joyce Powzyk	Non-fiction	2	26	14
1/../91	How to Fink...	Stephen Manes	Non-fiction	6	44	15
1/22/91	The Lion the Witch and the Wardrobe	C.S. Lewis	fiction	1	230	16
12/..	Yukon Ho! Calvin and Hobbes	Bill Watterson	fiction-comic	3	126	17
12/1/91	The Authoritative...	Bill Watterson	fiction-comic	3	253	18
12/3/91	Sunday Book	Bill Watterson	fiction-comic	3	127	19
1/4/92	Calvin & Hobbes	Bill Watterson	fiction-comic	3	126	20
	Scientific Progress Goes Boink	Bill Watterson	fiction-comic	4	126	21
1/15/92	Prince Caspian	C.S. Lewis	fiction	7	230	22

Date	Title	Author	Genre	Rate	Pages	
1/26/92	The Voyage of the Dawn Treader	C.S. Lewis	fiction	6	216	23
1/30/92	The Spanish Kid Dis.	Hahn	fiction	6	128	24
2/10/92	Abels Island	William Steig	fiction	4	120	25
2/10/92	Germs make me sick!	Melvin Berger	Non-fiction	3	32	26
3/6/92	The Trumpet of the swan	E.B. White	fiction	4	210	27
3/8/92	The BFG	Roald Dahl	fiction	5	218	28
3/10/92		Ontario Science	Non-fiction	4	123	29
3/10/92	Authoritative Calvin and Hobbes	Bill Watterson	fiction	3	253	30
4/23/92	The world of Andy Capp	Reg Smythe	fiction	7	300?	31
4/23/92	Incognito Mosquito	E.A. Hass	fiction	6	104	32
4/3/92	House of Danger	R.A. Montgomery	choose your adventure	3	106	33
5/10/92	Snow Treasure	Marie McSwigan	Historical fiction	5	156	34
5/11/92	A drop of Blood		non-fiction	1	36	35
5/13/92	Sickley Colors		non-fiction	3	54	36
5/14/92	The Human Body		non-fiction	4	42	37
6/2/92	Calvin & Hobbes	Bill Watterson	fiction	5	127	38
6/4/92	Adams family		fiction	3	72	39
						40
						41
						42
						43
						44
						45

List of books read

7. Text Samples

A text sample is a photocopy of a page or two of a book that a student has read. It can be a page from a book that was read and discussed on audiotape or a page the student chose for a particular reason, such as the vivid vocabulary.

Use text samples to document the type of literature your students are reading and its degree of difficulty. When students select text samples for their portfolios, ask them to write the reasons for their selections.

8. Lists of Books Read

Have students keep records of books read in and out of school, noting the title, author, and illustrator of each book and any of the following additional information: number of pages read, type of literature, date of entry, date student completed the book, and difficulty level.

At the end of a grading period, students can make graphs illustrating information about the books they read. For example, they can graph the number of books read each month or the number of fiction and nonfiction books read during the quarter.

By keeping such a list of books, students learn more about the type of literature they are reading and develop responsibility in record-keeping. If your students include book lists in their portfolios, have them evaluate their lists (noting the variety of literature read) and set goals based on their observations. For example, in examining her list, a student might realize that all of the books are part of a series, such as *The Babysitters Club* by Anne Martin (Scholastic). This student might set a goal to read books by other authors, including nonfiction. (*See page 103 for a sample reproducible List of Books Read record sheet.*)

Name. Danny   Date April 9, 1992

Student Comments	Goals	Teacher Comments
I've improved my writing and reading through the year.	Writing	What do you think your portfolio show.
My stories are much longer.	I will put more information in my non-fiction stories.	
I wrote more than one page in my journal.		
I've started to use commas in my writing.		
I can write a letter correctly.	Reading	
I've I used more describing words in my stories.	I will read one non-fiction book a week.	

Record of a portfolio conference

9. Records of Portfolio Conferences

A portfolio conference is a chance for teacher and student to discuss the portfolio and reflect on the student's goals and accomplishments. This dialogue helps the student recognize his strengths and improvements as a reader and writer. It's also an opportunity for students to discuss past goals and set new goals for the upcoming quarter. At the same time, you gain valuable information about the student's growth. To include records of conferences in students' portfolios, record student comments on conference record sheets. Place completed record sheets in students' portfolios. (*See Chapter 5, pages 49–50, for detailed information on conducting portfolio conferences. See pages 104–105 for sample conference sheets.*)

Engaging Students in Self-Evaluation and Goal-Setting

"I can't believe the improvement I've made in writing math responses! Look at what I wrote the first quarter, and now look at what I wrote this quarter. I write smaller. All my letters go the right way, and I can explain how to find area and perimeter."
(Amanda, 2nd grade)

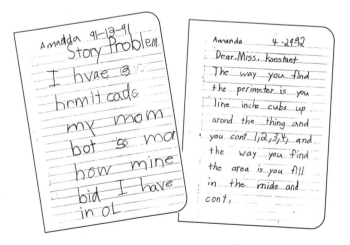

If you take a look at the two student samples above, you will probably understand second-grader Amanda's enthusiasm as she self-evaluates her improvement in writing in her learning log. Portfolios give students an active role in self-evaluation and goal-setting and let them see actual progress from one period to the next. When students are involved in evaluating their own work and setting goals for themselves, they take more responsibility for their learning and become motivated to achieve their goals.

Students at any grade level—even as early as kindergarten—can learn how to evaluate their own work and set goals. Following is a step-by-step guideline for teaching self-evaluation and goal-setting strategies that the students can use as they become independent lifelong learners. You can modify the suggestions to meet the needs of your students. For example, you may want to provide additional practice samples for self-evaluation (step 2) before students actually evaluate their own work (step 3). Keep in mind that as with learning any new skill, students will need practice, reminders, and reinforcement to become proficient at evaluating their own work.

Teaching Self-Evaluation and Goal-Setting in Writing

Step 1: Developing Criteria for Effective Writing

Before students can evaluate their own writing, they need to understand standards of good writing. Therefore, the criteria for effective writing must be established by you and your students. It is important to involve your students in this process. Begin by gathering writing samples that illustrate skills and content that are appropriate for your particular grade level. (You might use student writing samples from a previous year or generate some yourself.) Display the samples on an overhead projector.

After reading the samples, invite students to brainstorm with you about each sample. Ask: Why is this an effective piece of writing? Record students responses on chart paper. At first your students may only note the mechanics of writing. You will need to guide them in identifying the criteria in the areas of composing and style. Use the criteria charts shown here only for ideas. As you develop criteria with your students, chart the responses in their words. (*See pages 110–111 for sample criteria charts for effective writing.*)

Develop additional lessons and add to the chart as opportunities arise. In one fifth-grade classroom, for example, the teacher observed some students writing run-on sentences. To address this problem, she presented a mini-lesson contrasting a paragraph containing well-written sentences with a paragraph containing run-on sentences. At the conclusion of the lesson, students had a clearer understanding of sentence structure. They were also able to add several items about sentence structure to their criteria list.

This criteria chart will become an ongoing teaching tool in your classroom. Expand on it throughout the year as students' needs dictate and encourage students to consult the list frequently whenever they write.

Step 2: Teaching Self-Evaluation

Toward the end of the grading period, present lessons that simulate self-evaluation. First, give small groups of students a copy of a writing sample similar to those initially used to develop the criteria chart. Have each group use the criteria chart to write an evaluation that states the strengths of the sample. Each group shares positive comments about the sample with the class. Encourage the other students to give feedback about each group's evaluation.

Self-evaluation and goal card

> Charles   June 3
>
> This piece shows my teacher and my parents I can get information from reading books. It shows that I can plan with a chart and revise a lot. It shows that I can use a dictionary and a thesaurus properly. It also shows I can make my paragraphs flow.
>
> Goal: In my next piece of writing I hope to use a wider variety of sentences.

Following this small group activity, give each child a copy of another sample. Again, have each student use the criteria chart to write an evaluation of the strengths of the sample. Invite students to share their comments with the class. Again, you and your students give feedback about the evaluations.

Step 3: Practicing Self-Evaluation

Now students are ready to select their own pieces of writing to evaluate. Allowing students to choose their own pieces gives them ownership of their portfolios. Again, encourage them to refer to the criteria chart to help them identify strengths in the selections they choose. Instruct students to write these positive remarks on comment cards and attach the cards to their writing samples. You might ask them to answer questions such as: What did I learn? What did I do well? The value of portfolios increases when students reflect on the pieces they choose for inclusion. When students have more experience reflecting on their writing, it is easier for them to discover what they can do. At first, the criteria charts help them with the process, but as they practice and gain confidence, they will need fewer prompts from the teacher and the charts.

Step 4: Introducing Goal-Setting

Once students are familiar with self-evaluation in writing, you can introduce goal-setting. In self-evaluations, students look for strengths in their writing samples. In goal-setting, students identify areas for improvement. Depending on the criteria identified in your classroom, students might analyze mechanics of writing, syntax, style, flow, organization, cohesion, and so on. The areas of need the students discover can become their goal.

Help students understand how to set goals that are both specific and realistic by sharing humorous examples of reading and writing goals such as, "My goal is to read a thousand books in a week." Encourage students to recognize that while the goal is specific—it does state a definite number of books to be read—it is not realistic.

Step 5: Teaching Goal-Setting

Once students understand the meaning of goal-setting, return to one of the first writing samples used to develop criteria for effective writing. Together, brainstorm areas of need for that sample. Remind students to refer to the criteria chart to determine how the sample could be improved.

Have students write goals as if the sample were their own. If a sample seems lacking in descriptive vocabulary, a student might write: "My goal is to make my writings more interesting. I am going to do this by using vivid words."

Give small groups of students the second writing sample used in step 2. This time, have students identify areas of need in the sample and state corresponding goals. Let groups share and discuss their findings with one another. Remind students to consider whether each goal is specific and realistic.

45

Step 6: Applying Goal-Setting Skills to Student Samples

The final phase of goal-setting training occurs when students set goals for their own writing. Have students return to the writing samples they selected and self-evaluated. Students use the criteria chart to analyze their samples and to set goals. Have them record their goals on comment cards and place the cards and samples in their portfolios.

Teaching Self-Evaluation and Goal-Setting in Written Responses to Literature

In addition to self-evaluating their writings, students will also evaluate and set goals for written responses to literature they are reading. Students read for a variety of purposes, and their responses should reflect that. For example, a student may compare herself to a character, discuss an author's style of writing, or explain a conflict and how it was resolved. These written responses show that the students are active readers who can express their ideas about the literature they are reading.

To self-evaluate these responses, students need to be aware of the criteria for effective responses to literature. As a class, develop a criteria chart for effective reading responses. Follow the same procedures outlined on page 44 (*Step 1: Developing Criteria for Effective Writing*), substituting samples of written responses to literature for the

writing samples. Continue following the plan outlined in Steps 2–6 to teach students how to self-evaluate and set goals, again, substituting samples of written responses to literature for the writing samples in each step. (*See pages 112–113 for sample criteria charts for written responses to literature.*)

Teaching Self-Evaluation and Goal-Setting in Written Responses in the Content Areas

With students, develop criteria for writing effective responses to learning in the content areas. Students use these to self-evaluate their learning-log entries and to set goals for improvement. Apply the same methods described for teaching self-evaluation and goal setting in writing beginning on page 44. Simply substitute samples from the learning logs for the writing samples. (*See pages 114–115 for sample criteria charts for learning logs.*)

Student's self-evaluation and goal card

Teacher and students discuss status of attaining goals.

❖ **TEACHING TIP** ❖

Display criteria charts for writing, reading responses, and content-area responses in your classroom. Encourage students to refer to them as they work. As students become accustomed to using the charts, they'll gain independence in their own learning and continually challenge themselves to improve as readers and writers.

Keeping Up with Goals

During a portfolio conference, an upper-elementary student was asked if he had accomplished the goals he had set for himself. He replied, "I just thought the goals were something I had to write down. I didn't know that I really had to do it." Students need to be reminded of their goals and the importance of working to achieve them on a regular basis. You can encourage them to work toward their goals by periodically meeting with small groups to review students' progress. Ask students to share their plans for meeting goals by the end of the quarter. Invite them to offer suggestions on ways their classmates can accomplish their goals.

Following these meetings, ask students to restate in writing how they are working to accomplish their goals. Students might, for example, write letters to the teacher explaining their goals and their plans of action. This process reinforces the importance of setting realistic goals and working to achieve them. Finally, remember that students need time to work on their goals! A second-grade student explicitly expressed this need in a letter to her teacher following their mid-quarter conference:

> Dear Mrs. Laase,
> My goal is to give a book talk evry week. I cannt becauz you arent doing book talks.
> Love, Mandi

Student letter on the status of her goal

Often, several students will identify the same goal. This is a good opportunity to plan mini-lessons for flexible groups based on their needs. Incorporating students' goals and your curriculum objectives into lesson plans fosters a student-centered classroom.

10/26

Cathryn, this reading log entry shows that you are able to write and tell how a character feels. You also told why you thought he would be scared.

Mrs. Laase

10/29

Aaron, this entry from your cricket diary shows that you can use scientific words when you write about a cricket. You also remembered to date your entry, which is so important when you keep a diary.

Mrs. Cooper

Teacher Evaluations

Your evaluations of students' strengths, as exemplified in their portfolio samples, are an integral part of the portfolio program. These evaluations can provide valuable information about your students' abilities. They also serve as reinforcement for students, letting them know what you see that they do well, and helping them learn new areas to explore in their own evaluations.

Comments may vary in length, but like student self-evaluations, they should be relevant to a specific sample and be stated in a concise, positive manner—that is, the comments should note what the student can do well. Write your comments after the students have evaluated and set goals on each sample. Because the student is the owner of the portfolio, address your comments to him or her. Write evaluative comments on cards or on pieces of paper and attach to pertinent samples. Three sample teacher evaluations follow.

5/29

Charles, this writing sample shows that you know how to use the writing process. You can research a topic and organize the data on a chart. Your draft shows that you added information as well as deleted parts. You also revised the order of some sections. You can write a variety of interesting sentences in paragraphs that flow. Your well-organized writing clearly explains the differences in the north and south prior to the Civil War.

Mrs. Clemmons

You may be wondering if you could use checklists in place of writing narrative comments. Although checklists may appear to be a quicker assessment tool, they can't compare with written evaluations that are individualized to reflect each student's strengths. As in learning any new skill, writing these evaluations will take more time at first, but as you gain experience, the process moves along more quickly.

Mrs. Cooper and Emily hold a portfolio conference.

Portfolio Conferences

The evaluation and goal-setting process culminates in portfolio conferences because they are a way of helping students learn more about their strengths and refine their goals. Conferences will help you to learn more about your students and how they perceive their learning. You and your students are collaborators in the evaluation process.

Portfolio conferences are typically held during the latter part of a quarter or marking period. Since each conference takes about ten to fifteen minutes, allow approximately two weeks to complete them. You'll find that you can hold a few portfolio conferences each day while the rest of the class is working independently or in small groups on reading and writing activities. Just like reading and writing conferences, portfolio conferences become a part of the routine in a reading and writing classroom.

Still, you might consider enlisting and training outside resources such as administrators, resource teachers, colleagues, and parents to help during this time. Assistants can work with other students as needed while you hold conferences. You might also train volunteers in conducting portfolio conferences to reduce the number of conferences you conduct and to provide a different perspective on what students are learning.

Before conferring with a student, take a few minutes to review the portfolio so that you can open the conference with positive comments. You might, for example, compliment the student's organization of the portfolio, or the thoughtful selection of pieces, and mention how you agree with the student's evaluative comments. Continue the conference by asking the student to share her portfolio by discussing the contents and by reflecting on her reading and writing growth. Remember, the conference is not an inquisition by the teacher; rather it is a shared discussion with the student, who is an active participant. If you need to encourage a student's participation in the conference, direct the discussion by asking questions such as:

❖ What do you do when you are reading to help you understand the content?

❖ What can you do well in writing?

❖ What does this piece tell about you as a reader and writer?

❖ What kinds of books do you like to read? Why?

- ❖ How does your reading help you in writing?
- ❖ How are you achieving the goals you set for yourself last quarter?

As you prepare for the conference, you might want to make use of a conference sheet. (*See pages 104–105 for sample conference sheets.*) On it, you can record questions and comments that will help students recognize their strengths and improvements as readers and writers. During the conference, add student comments to the sheet. Bring the portfolio conference to a close by asking the student to state overall reading and writing goals for the next quarter or marking period. Some students may need guidance to set realistic and specific goals. Record these goals on the conference sheet and place it in the portfolio.

> *"When you set goals for portfolios you get use to it, so you just set goals in class and in sports."* (Joshua, 5th grade)
>
> *"What I like about goals is when you can't do something and it is bothering you, you can make a goal. When you have a goal you can learn to do it and it reminds you of it and you are happy about yourself."* (Matt, 2nd grade)

Record of a portfolio conference

Record of Portfolio Conference   Student's Name __Karen__

Date __March 31__

Teacher's Comments	Student's Comments	Goals

* You have met your first quarter reading goal for reading non-fiction books. I can see you enjoy historical fiction and non-fiction.
  Goals from 2nd qtr:
* Did you meet your 2nd quarter goal of reading one or two hours a day? **Yes.**
* Which topic did you research? **Alzheimers.**
* How has your revision improved? Are you satisfied with your paragraphing? (See comments)
	I learned that reading biographies can help me in social studies. When I read about the person in my social studies book I have a greater understanding because of my own personal reading on that person. It helps me with the data retrieval chart because I know the information.
	  Reading also helps me with writing. I know a lot more for my web and draft. My ideas are clearer. I like Jean Fritz's books because she finds out the truth. I like the way she makes her books sound like the person whom the book is about wrote the book himself! I try to imitate this in my writing.
	  I've improved in my writing this past quarter I've been writing more about the subject, and I don't use run-on sentences. I can stay on a topic now, and I can write paragraphs.
	  I think that the think-aloud strategy that's worked best for me is rereading. I used it in <u>Island of The Blue Dolphins</u>.
	  Now I can read non-fiction books and biographies. I'm writing better responses because I'm asking questions, predicting, and putting myself in the character's place.
		* To read 4 non-fiction book and 5 fiction books
		* To write more clear reading responses
		  * I will read more of the book during reading time
		  * I will reread my writing and look at the reading journal charts.
		* In taping, I will be more prepared for my book talks.
		  * I will practice at home
		* I will use more reading strategies: reread; predict and ask questions. If I can't find the answer, I'll write it in my reading response and find it the next day.

Setting Up Your Portfolio Program: A Step-by-Step Guide

Once you have become familiar with what is involved in implementing portfolio assessment, a condensed presentation of that information can help you move smoothly through the year from one phase to the next—from gathering the supplies you'll need to begin your portfolio program to selecting samples to send on to your students' next teachers. Whether you are teaching in a self-contained classroom or in a departmental setting, you can adapt this to meet your needs.

The pages that follow present such a framework. A supplies checklist includes brief descriptions of the basic materials you'll want to have on hand to implement your portfolio program. You might want to copy and save these pages for easy reference as you prepare your classroom each year. The Year-Long Plan presents information contained in previous chapters of this book in abbreviated form. So if you have a quick question, about including audiotape recordings, for example, you can quickly locate that information in the first-quarter section of this four-quarter plan. If you like, you can copy and post these pages to help in pacing your portfolio program each quarter. Through your guidance, the students will quickly learn how to maintain their own portfolios.

Portfolio Assessment:
Suggested Supplies

☐ **composition books**
Students can keep reading journals and learning logs in these books. Having responses for each of these components in one place facilitates the process of reflecting and choosing samples for portfolios.

☐ **writing folders**
A pocket folder helps students keep all stages of their writing samples together.

☐ **audiocassette tapes/videocassette tapes**
Ask the students, the school, or the PTA to provide individual tapes for recording student work.

☐ **tape recorder/video camera**
This equipment should be available for use as needed.

☐ **file folders**
A letter-size or legal-size file folder is recommended for housing the contents of each student's portfolio.

☐ **large boxes or crates**
Boxes and crates are ideal for storing portfolios. File cabinets may be dangerous for students to use. Hanging files help keep portfolios organized.

☐ **index cards**
Students and teachers can write their evaluations on these cards.

☐ **manila envelopes**
Six-by-nine-inch manila envelopes are recommended for storing audiotapes. Twelve-by-fifteen-inch manila envelopes are ideal for transporting portfolios home.

☐ **chart paper**
Sheets of tag board or paper are useful for charting criteria. The sheets need to be large enough so that the print can easily be seen by all students.

☐ **construction paper**
Use twelve-by-eighteen-inch construction paper to make mini-folders for each quarter and for students' baseline samples. Students simply fold the construction paper in half and insert work for each quarter. Color-coding folders can assist students in organizing work. For example, students might use red for their first quarter work, green for second quarter, and so on.

Aaron looks at his portfolio.

A Yearlong Plan

First Quarter

1. Select components.

What components will students include in their portfolios? You and your students determine which components suit your needs. To help students include samples representing each component, post a list of portfolio components. (*See Chapter 4, page 35–42, for more information on choosing components.*)

2. Introduce students to the concept of portfolios.

Invite an artist to share a professional portfolio with students. This will help students to understand how portfolios can showcase their work.

3. Personalize file folders.

To emphasize that the portfolio belongs to the student, have each child decorate the outside of a file folder that will become the portfolio. This is the first step in personalizing the folder.

4. Inform parents.

Share information with parents about the use of portfolios as a classroom assessment tool. This can be done at back-to-school night and through letters. (*See page 95 for sample reproducible letter to parents.*)

5. Collect baseline samples.

As early in the school year as possible, collect baseline samples—students' first pieces of work in each of the portfolio component areas.

6. File baseline samples.

Baseline samples are the first samples students place in their portfolios. Students can begin to organize their portfolios by placing baseline samples in mini-folders. Have students use 12-by-18-inch pieces of construction paper to construct the folders. All students should use the same color paper to indicate that these folders contain baseline samples. If you arrange portfolios alphabetically, it helps to number them so that when students return folders to the storage crate, they can check placement by numerical order.

7. Show students how to keep records of the literature they read.

Create a form for students to record book information. (*See page 103 for sample book recording form.*) You might print the form on brightly colored paper to help students differentiate it from other forms. Use a different color each quarter. Another method is to have students reserve a small section in their reading journals to record titles, authors, pages, dates of completion, or other information about literature read. Students can affix a tab to this section to facilitate access.

8. Develop criteria charts.
Using student samples, have students brainstorm and chart with you the criteria for various types of writing: expository, narrative, responses to literature and to learning in the content areas, and so on. Add criteria to the charts as students acquire new skills throughout the year. It's important to develop new criteria with students each year, because the process helps students in writing for different purposes and assists them in self-evaluating and goal-setting. (*See Chapter 5, page 44, for guidelines on developing criteria. See pages 110–116 for sample criteria charts.*)

9. Prepare for audiocassette taping.
Sometime during the first quarter, have students select books that they will read for audiotape recordings. Invite parent volunteers to assist with taping. To facilitate the process, prepare a list of instructions.

❖ Check that the tape recorder works.

❖ Note the numbers where each recording begins and ends (using the same tape recorder throughout the year ensures that the counter numbers are consistent).

❖ Check that the child can be heard on the recording before proceeding with the reading sample.

❖ Make certain that the tape is on the proper side.

Store completed audiotapes in small manila envelopes. Record the following information on each student's envelope: date of the recording, title of the selection, and the beginning and ending counter numbers. (*See page 109 for clip-and-post directions for audiotape recordings.*)

Volunteer assists Meghan in taping a book.

Emergent learners draw pictures as a response to a story.

10. Teach students to self-evaluate and to set goals.

Approximately three weeks before the end of the grading period, instruct students on self-evaluation and goal-setting. Use selected work samples to show students how to apply the criteria listed on the charts to each writing sample being evaluated. Teach students how to self-evaluate their writing, their written responses to literature, and their learning-log entries. After practicing this procedure several times, most students will be ready to evaluate their own samples and set goals. This method for teaching self-evaluation and setting goals can be modified to fit all of the portfolio components. (*See Chapter 5, pages 44–46, for guidelines on teaching self-evaluation and goal-setting. See page 108 for sample student chart: How to Evaluate Portfolios.*)

11. Provide time for students to select samples for portfolios.

Immediately following the lesson on self-evaluating, have students study their work and select a piece of writing to include in their portfolios. Encourage students to use the criteria chart as a guide for identifying what the samples show they can do. Next have them find areas for improvement and set goals. Have students write their evaluations and goals on index cards or pieces of paper and attach them to the samples. Repeat this process when students select samples from their reading journals and learning logs.

12. Provide time for students to self-evaluate and set goals for other components in their portfolios.

Give students time to graph the types of literature they are reading, to listen to their audiotapes, and to view their videos. As with writing samples, have students write self-evaluations and set goals for these other components.

13. Think about including a handwriting sample.

Although a handwriting sample may not be listed as one of your portfolio components, you may want to include one each quarter. Good handwriting is usually not high on students' priorities when they are thinking, creating, and writing. The best way to get handwriting samples is to ask students to include an original sentence written in their best handwriting. (*See page 107 for sample handwriting evaluation card.*)

14. Consider including an art sample.
Students often use the visual arts—paintings, drawings, sculptures, collages—to respond to literature. For emergent learners in particular, art is a way to respond to a read-aloud or to a story they read. Students can evaluate art samples by writing about how the art relates to the story. Emergent learners can dictate evaluations or complete a teacher-prepared form such as "I can_____." If a visual art sample is too large to be placed in the portfolio, take a picture and include it.

15. Write your evaluations of student portfolio samples.
Once students have self-evaluated their selections and set goals, you can write your own evaluative comments for each portfolio piece. Your responses should reflect student strengths and be relevant to the specific samples. Write your comments on cards or on pieces of paper and attach them to the samples.

16. Have students organize their portfolios.
After students select and evaluate samples, have them organize their portfolios by making mini-folders from construction paper for first-quarter work. As with baseline samples, have all students use the same color for first-quarter work, a different color for second quarter, and so on. Students can write a table of contents for each quarter's samples. Have students place first-quarter folders behind their baseline sample folders.

17. Conduct end-of-the-quarter portfolio conferences.
As students complete their selections and evaluations, confer with individual students one at a time. Allow ten to fifteen minutes for each conference—or about two to three weeks to meet with all of your students. (*See Chapter 5, pages 49–50, for more information on portfolio conferences.*)

Students organize their portfolios.

Mrs. Laase teaches a mini-lesson.

18. Focus on students' goals.

To stress the importance of attaining goals, have parent volunteers write students' goals on cards, laminate them if possible, and affix the cards to students' desks. This way, the goals are always visible to both you and the students.

19. Share portfolios at parent/teacher conferences.

Use students' reading and writing portfolios to help parents understand what their children have accomplished. Discuss how self-evaluations and goals actively involve children in their learning. (*See Chapter 3, page 30, for more information on parent/teacher conferences.*)

20. Send portfolios home.

Send portfolios home with report cards. To prevent any of the contents from being lost, place each student's portfolio in a large envelope. On the outside of the envelope write a statement requesting that the entire portfolio be returned to school. To help parents better understand their child's portfolio, include an explanatory letter about the contents. If you don't have parent/teacher conferences at this time, include an explanatory letter about portfolios in general, as well. (*See pages 96–97 for reproducible explanatory letters to parents.*)

Second Quarter

1. Develop mini-lessons.

Use student evaluations, student goals, your observations, and school curriculum guidelines to develop mini-lessons that address students' needs as they arise. Encourage students to apply what they learn in these lessons to improve their reading and writing. Use children's literature, students' writing, or your own original samples as part of the material for instruction.

Parent and teacher (Mrs. Areglado) share a portfolio.

2. Add to class criteria charts.

As you teach new skills, have students add criteria to the charts.

3. Conduct mid-quarter goal conferences.

Meet periodically with small groups to assist students in working to attain their goals. Discuss how they are accomplishing their goals and share strategies for remembering and attaining goals. Have students write about what they have accomplished thus far and how they will meet their goals. Remind students frequently about the importance of attaining their goals.

4. Make audiotape recordings.

This second recording follows first-quarter tapings on students' audiocassettes. Use the same tape recorder and fast-forward to the number on the counter that indicates where the last recording ended (as noted on the envelope). Follow the same procedures you used first quarter.

5. Review self-evaluation and goal-setting process.

Before students select work samples for their portfolios, review procedures for self-evaluation and goal-setting.

6. Provide time for students to select and evaluate samples and to set goals.

Offer guidance as students select samples to be included in their portfolios. Encourage them to use the criteria charts as they write evaluations and set new goals.

7. Include teacher evaluations.

After students have evaluated their selections, write and attach your own positive comments to the samples.

8. Organize second-quarter portfolio materials.

Choose a third color of construction paper to make mini-folders for students' second-quarter samples. (Baseline samples are one color, first-quarter samples are a second color, and so on.) Students may write and include a table of contents before adding these folders to their portfolios.

9. Conduct student/teacher portfolio conferences.

Begin to confer with students as they complete their tape recordings, evaluations, and goal-setting. Plan on completing about three conferences a day, unless you have outside help to conduct additional ones. Allow two to three weeks to complete conferences with all of your students.

10. Include a letter to parents in students' portfolios.

Write a letter to parents explaining the contents of the portfolios. This letter will guide parents through their child's portfolio. It will help them to focus on the samples and the evaluations and to understand the portfolio as an authentic assessment tool. (*See pages 96–97 for sample letters to parents.*)

11. Send portfolios home.

Place portfolios in the large manila envelopes and send them home with report cards. If you are requesting parent feedback, include a questionnaire in each student's portfolio. (*See pages 99–101 for sample questionnaires.*)

Katie and Beth are portfolio partners.

Third Quarter

1. Follow the same procedures as you did during the second quarter.

At this time of the school year, you'll probably notice that students are becoming very comfortable with the portfolio process. Many have experienced success in attaining their goals and eagerly look for samples that show how they have reached those goals. They are more readily using criteria charts to evaluate their work and are likely to go beyond evaluating spelling, handwriting, or mechanics to explain how they composed a piece of writing or why they enjoyed a particular author. You'll find that by now many students will move through the stages of developing portfolios more independently.

2. Invite parents to write letters to their child about the portfolio.

You might include a note when portfolios go home this quarter suggesting that parents respond to their child's portfolio in a letter to the child. You'll be delighted with the positive comments that parents write to their children. Success builds upon success—and portfolios are wonderful tools for developing this positive attitude.

Ahmed writes his evaluation.

Fourth Quarter

As with the first, second, and third quarters, students make tape recordings, select samples, and evaluate their work. But now, the goals they set are ones they want to achieve during the summer. Since it is the end of the school year, there are a few procedural changes.

1. Have each student evaluate a partner's portfolio samples.

Because of time constraints at the end of the year, you may choose to have students evaluate one another's fourth-quarter samples in place of your comments. You'll find that most students are able to do this now because not only are they experienced at writing evaluations, but they've also been reading your positive comments all year, which serve as models for them to follow.

Prepare students for this activity by reviewing the evaluation process. Remind them to read their portfolio partners' samples carefully and to use the criteria charts for assistance. Emphasize that comments must be positive and must tell what the samples show that their partners have learned and can do well. Have students

Janet shares her end-of-the-year portfolio letter with her teacher (Mrs. Laase).

write their comments on cards and attach them to the samples they evaluate. Rather than having students try to complete the evaluations in one day, set aside time for them to write one evaluation each day. (*See page 106 for portfolio partner guidelines.*)

2. Replace portfolio conferences with student letters.

In lieu of portfolio conferences at the end of the school year, ask students to write letters to you expressing their thoughts about how they have grown in reading and writing. Before they begin writing, encourage them to review their portfolios and reflect on the samples they have cho-sen. Have them brainstorm ideas to discuss in their letters, such as types of literature that they like to read or write, or improvements they've seen in reading and writing. Have students place these letters in their portfolios.

3. Select reading and writing portfolio samples to send to the next teachers. Send portfolios home with students.

At the close of school, portfolios can be sent with the students' records to the next teachers. If you're like most teachers, you probably don't have room to store additional sets of portfolios. Also, students have worked hard on their portfolios all year and naturally will want to keep them. Toward the end of the school year, copy a baseline writing sample and a fourth-quarter writing sample for each student. These comparative samples provide an authentic assessment of writing growth. Make copies of students' booklists to show levels of difficulty and variety of books read. Pass both writing samples and booklists on to students' next teachers.

Name Aaron   Date 6/10/92
Portfolio Partner
Danny can white non-fiction
story. Danny nos alot about
snakes. His hand witing is readed.
Danny did a very good job.

Portfolio partner evaluation

Questions and Answers

As we speak with teachers across the country, we hear many of the same questions again and again. You've probably found the answers to most of your questions in chapters 1 through 6. Are you still wondering about something? Here are some questions that may remain.

Q. Can I use portfolios with children of any age and ability?

A. The answer is a resounding yes! We have found using portfolios with children, from kindergarten to sixth grade, to be very successful. In our school, special-education and ESL students have also been included. Growth is evidenced by a comparison of baseline samples and later-in-the-year samples. Colleagues in the seventh through twelfth grades have also had impressive results.

Q. Can portfolios be used in a classroom that has a large number of students?

A. Our classes range from 23 to 30 students. If you follow the steps outlined in Chapter Seven, you will discover that you can use portfolios with any size class. Plan ahead so that all your students have time to select and evaluate samples, set goals, and get their portfolios ready to go home before you get involved with report cards.

Q. Is it okay to use checklists to evaluate students' portfolios instead of writing a comment for each portfolio entry?

A. There are a number of risks in using checklists to evaluate portfolio samples.

1. You may find yourself fitting the student to the checklist, thereby overlooking the talents of individual students.

2. You risk teaching to the checklist, consequently steering away from more creative and purposeful lesson plans.

3. By using lists developed by outside sources, you may not be addressing your students' specific needs.

Given the personal nature of portfolios, it only makes sense that teacher comments be personal as well.

Q. Can checklists be used for student self-evaluations?

A. Just as teacher checklists have limited use as an evaluative tool, so have student checklists. Students could work to achieve the limited number of tasks on a checklist, thereby discouraging both creativity and growth. The checklist itself may be viewed as just another task—reducing the self-evaluation process from one of ongoing learning and goal-setting to an exercise in simple mastery.

Q. How can I convince my building administrator that portfolio assessment can be an effective supplement to report cards?

A. First, you must be knowledgeable about the values of portfolio assessment so that you can present your administrator with information that is both convincing and factual. Explain that portfolio assessment helps build home-school connections, fostering student success. Share books and articles about portfolio assessment. Find out about other schools using portfolio assessment. *Portfolio News* regularly offers information about schools using portfolios (including names, addresses, and phone numbers). Arrange to visit one of these schools and invite your administrator to go with you. It's usually seeing portfolios in action that sells the program. So ask lots of questions! Invite several teachers to a staff meeting to talk about how they got started with portfolios. Finally, keep an eye out for conferences featuring workshops or sessions on portfolios. Encourage an administrator to attend.

Q. How can I encourage colleagues who are less than enthusiastic about portfolio assessment?

A. Typical arguments against using portfolios include: "I already have too much to do!" "But we still have to use report cards." "My students are too disorganized to keep portfolios." You'll be happy to hear that in our experience, once teachers get to know more about portfolios, enthusiasm quickly replaces concerns. You and those willing to listen and learn about portfolios can be catalysts for change.

Whether you're trying to encourage an individual teacher or an entire school, you'll find the following tips helpful.

1. Share and discuss articles and books about portfolios.

2. Show actual examples of reading and writing portfolios.

3. Invite colleagues to observe your program in action and to talk with your students about portfolios.

4. Bring a colleague along when you visit a school that is using portfolios.

5. Attend conferences with a colleague.

6. Invite speakers (including students and parents) to present information and ideas about portfolios.

7. Keep enthusiasm alive by continuing to be a resource for teachers in your building.

Q. I want to use portfolios, but my school requires letter grades at the end of each quarter. Will getting a letter grade for language arts and using reading and writing portfolios as an assessment tool send a mixed message to my students?

A. We are frequently asked this question, and it is a difficult one to answer. When conferring with students at portfolio conferences, we discuss their short-term goals and emphasize their efforts and progress as shown in the portfolio—regardless of the grade that is on their report cards. It has been our experience that a student's personal learning objectives eventually become more important to him or her than the grades on their report cards. For students motivated in this way, it is real learning—not a grade—that matters most.

Q. Why do you continue to use portfolios?

A. The students' enthusiasm and excitement make us want to continue to use portfolios. We do not see this excitement and enthusiasm generated by other assessment tools. Students' self-concepts are enhanced when they see the progress they are making. Through the use of portfolios, they are actively involved in the evaluation process as they self-evaluate their work and set goals for improvement. They take more responsibility for their learning because they are motivated to achieve their own goals. If your ultimate aim in education is to develop independent learners, there are few better ways than the use of portfolios.

Portfolio Snapshots: What's Inside

Throughout this book you have gotten glimpses of real students' portfolios. Here's a chance to get a better look. On the pages that follow, Jonathan, a second grader, and Alexis, a fifth grader, share their portfolios with you. A brief annotation tells a little bit about each piece.

The actual portfolios contain drafts, revisions, finished products with fancy covers, audiocassettes, and videocassettes—which we could not reproduce here. Still, by comparing selected samples from one quarter to the next, you'll be able to see the different components over time present pictures of how these students are growing in reading, writing, self-evaluation, and goal-setting.

JONATHAN'S PORTFOLIO
(PRIMARY: Second grade)

Baseline Samples

These samples were selected the first week of school to use as a baseline. This is the only time that Jonathan was not involved in selecting work to include in the portfolio.

Student's folder

Jonathan 9-5-91

Best Friend
Brian we play toga-
thr we are funny
togathr we bild with
Lego. He has Brown eyes.

Baseline reading-log sample

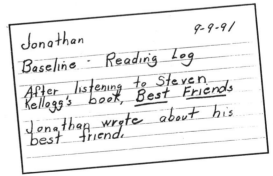

Jonathan   9-9-91
Baseline - Reading Log
After listening to Steven
Kellogg's book, Best Friends
Jonathan wrote about his
best friend.

Explanation of baseline reading-log sample

Jonathan 9-4-91

How to Be a
Nature Detective
Look for tracs in
the mud. Look
for slithr tracs
Holls in the grown-
d. Watar tracs.
The food that they eot

Keep up the good work.
You have wonderful ideas here.

Baseline learning-log sample

Jonathan   9-11-91

Baseline - Learning Log

After listening to several
nature books Jonathon wrote
about ways to be a nature
detective.

Explanation of baseline learning-log sample

Jonathan
Mrs. Laase.
Today is the first
day of school.

Baseline handwriting sample

Baseline

HANDWRITING   Jonathan 9/91

✓ well formed letters_____
✓ correct line placement_____
✓ good spacing_____
✓ no reversals_____
✓ capital letters used correctly_____

Baseline handwriting evaluation

Selections from Jonathan's First-Quarter Portfolio Components

In addition to components shown here, Jonathan included an audiotape recording of his reading, a sample page of a book he was reading, and the notes from his portfolio conference.

Reading-Log Sample

Jonathan chose to include a response to the book *Jimmy's Boa and the Big Splash Birthday* by Trinke Noble (Dial, 1989). Since this response was written early in the first-quarter, there is little growth when compared to the baseline sample. Although his evaluation is brief and not specific, Jonathan is becoming involved in evaluating his work.

Jonathan 9-13-91

I read, Jimmy's Boa and the Big splash Birthday I did et
Read all off it the time-
I wen't off I had Two
pagis left

Reading-log sample

Name Jonathan   Date 10-24-91
        Reading Log
I whote what I was suposta. I wrote with alot of confidence. goal I will read 3 more books by having more time.

Student evaluation

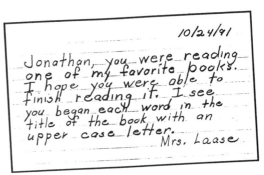

10/24/91

Jonathan, you were reading one of my favorite books. I hope you were able to finish reading it. I see you began each word in the title of the book with an upper case letter.
                    Mrs. Laase

Teacher evaluation

Record of Books Read

Jonathan kept a record of what he read each day during DEAR (Drop Everything and Read) time. Because it takes a while for students to develop the habit of recording what they read each day, it helps to regularly remind students about their booklists.

Reading record

Reading Record

Name Jonathan

Date	Title of what I am reading
9-4-91	The day Jimmys Boa Ate the wash
9-4-91	GIANT Dinosaurs
9-5-91	RoGeR RaBBit
9-5-91	Round TRIP
9-6-91	Beans in the Night
9-10-91	the Beginning of the eARth
9-11-91	the day Jimmys Boa eat the wash
	TyRome the HoRRiBLe
9-19-91	GiGGLes and GaGs GRoaneRs
9-20-91	Haunted Harbor
9-25-91	Giant din

Learning Log

Jonathan evaluated this math sample in terms of mechanics, but his goal shows that he is concerned about the content of his writing. He states that he wants to be more scientific and to write in more detail. The teacher's evaluation reflects strengths in both those areas: Jonathan knows how to use commas in a list and he understands the concept of even numbers.

Learning-log sample

Jonathan 10-18-91
Even # 398
You recunis a even like by looking in the ones place wich is the end number. It is very simpal no mada if the nuber is like 3000 you now its even nuber. The even nuber a 0,2,4,6, 8, is in the one's Place.

Name Jonathan   Date 10-25-91

Learning Log

I think I did a good job I rememberd periods goal I will try to be more scientific. I will try to write with detail.

Student evaluation

10-25-91

Jonathan, you did a great job explaining how you recognize an even number. You wrote in sentences so it was easy to understand. I see you know that you put commas between numbers when you list them. Mrs. Laase

Teacher evaluation

Writing Sample

Jonathan writes in his journal every day. Both his evaluation and goal-setting show concern for the mechanics of writing—he says he uses periods at the end of sentences, but also indicates that he is going to improve on this skill by slowly rereading his work and making necessary corrections.

Writing sample

10-10-91 Jonathan

Yesterday I played spis with Brian. these are the thing we yousd, A grabr and a fake nife and a gun We played for a sort time. Then my dad bilt a nothar swinging thing. It hort my hends. Then I went in and wacht my dad work on the cnputer. Then I wacht Tv. It was a rety fun day.

Date 10-24-91

Name Jonathan   Writing Sample.
I can put periods at the end of my sentences. I can put upper case letters at the beging of my sentences. Goal I'll put periods and quostcan marks where they belon by going over my story slowly.

Student evaluation

Jonathan,   10/24/92
This writing sample from your journal shows that you can tell about things in the order that they happened. You also wrote two interesting sentences about the swing. You left spaces between your words so it was easy to read.
                    Mrs. Laase

Teacher evaluation

Selections from Jonathan's Second-Quarter Portfolio Components

In addition to the following five samples, Jonathan included a tape of his reading, a text sample, a list of books read, and a letter from his teacher explaining the contents of his portfolio.

Reading Log

Jonathan's evaluation of his response to a book he read indicates that he is still concerned about mechanics. The teacher's evaluation points out what he can do: He can have one character in a book write to another character. Through the teacher's comment, Jonathan can see other ways of evaluating his work.

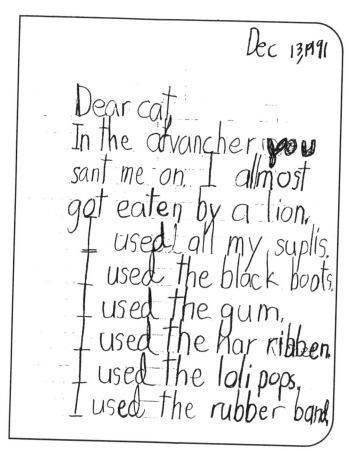

Dec 13,1991

Dear cat,
In the advancher you
sant me on, I almost
got eaten by a lion,
I used all my suplis,
I used the black boots,
I used the gum,
I used the har ribben,
I used the loli pops,
I used the rubber band,

Reading-log sample

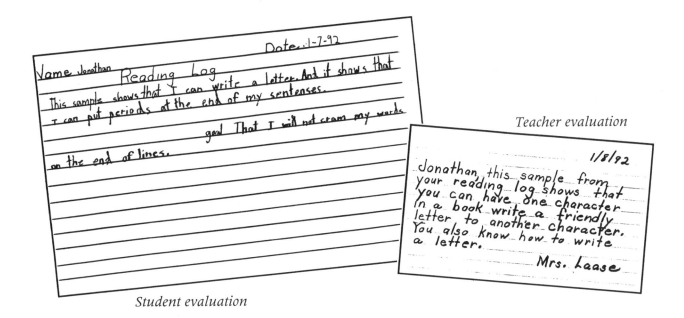

Date: 1-7-92

Name Jonathan   Reading Log
This sample shows that I can write a letter. And it shows that
I can put periods at the end of my sentenses.
goal That I will not cram my words
on the end of lines.

Student evaluation

Teacher evaluation

1/8/92
Jonathan, this sample from
your reading log shows that
you can have one character
in a book write a friendly
letter to another character.
You also know how to write
a letter.

Mrs. Laase

Learning Log

Notice how the teacher's first-quarter comment about using commas now appears in Jonathan's evaluation. He is still concerned about mechanics but notices that he has reached a goal from last quarter—he used scientific words in his response to the study of weighing with a balance.

Learning-log sample

> 12-4-11 Jonathan — Jonathan
> what I learned
> about balancing
>
> I made a graph
> to wey thing like
> Sinker, ball, marble,
> tile, spange, clothes-
> pin, spool, sautck tip,
> angle iron and washer
> we wayed them too.
> we wayed 10 gm

Student evaluation

> Name Jonathan   Date 12-4-91
>   Learning Log
> I remembered to put commas for a list. I put periods at
> the end of my sentenses. I used sinentific words.
>   goal That I make my storys a
> little more interesting

Teacher evaluation

> Jonathan   12/9/
> When you made your list
> of things you weighed you
> used commas to separate them.
> Your illustration of the balance
> goes nicely with your discussion
> about what you learned about
> balancing. Nice job.

Writing Sample

This was the last portfolio sample Jonathan evaluated this quarter. Note the growth in his ability to write an evaluation. He doesn't mention mechanics. Instead, he is concerned with the style of his writing.

Writing sample (first draft)

Writing sample

Teacher evaluation

Student evaluation

Handwriting sample

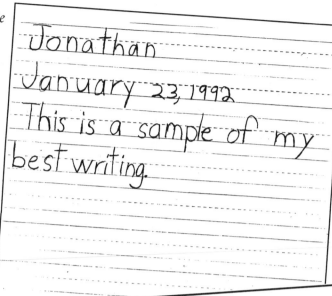

Jonathan

January 23, 1992

This is a sample of my best writing.

Handwriting Sample

Parents and students frequently have difficulty differentiating between handwriting and writing. When handwriting is messy (as it frequently is in a draft), it is difficult to focus on the content. This handwriting sample shows that Jonathan can write neatly when necessary. The statement attached to the sample explains why good handwriting is not always high on his priority list.

Handwriting evaluation

Handwriting

The children write daily in their journals. They respond to assignments in their reading and learning logs. They create original stories. Good handwriting is not high on their priority when they are thinking, creating, and writing. As a result their work does not look as beautiful as it may sound.

This is a sample of handwriting when writing neatly is the highest priority.

- ✔ well formed letters_____
- ✔ correct line placement_____
- ✔ good spacing_____
- ✔ no reversals_____
- ✔ capital letters used correctly_____

Portfolio Conference Record Sheet

The questions on the conference record sheet helped Jonathan's teacher encourage his participation in the discussion. Jonathan's comments were recorded on this sheet. He was truthful when he wrote that he had not reached his writing goal for that quarter.

Portfolio conference record sheet

Jonathan

PORTFOLIO CONFERENCE
SECOND QUARTER

<u>READING</u>

What was your goal and did you reach it? I will read 2 non-fiction books. Yes I reached it. One book I read was about animals. I can't remember the other one.

What was one of your favorite books you have read recently?
<u>Fool of the World and the Flying Ship</u>

If you come to a difficult word when you are reading what do you do?
-I use letter sounds.
-I cut it up into little words.

<u>WRITING</u>

What was your goal and did you reach it? I will reread my work to see if it makes sense.
"No, sometimes when we talked about what I wrote you would ask if I read it."
When you took your learning log home what did you tell your parents about your writing?
They asked me questions and I told them about it.

What will be your goal for next quarter?

Reading
I will read 4 non-fiction books. I will write the names on my reading record.

Writing
I will keep writing like my clown story.

Selections from Jonathan's Third-Quarter Portfolio Components

In his reading log, learning log, and writing components, Jonathan still mentions that he is mastering mechanics. At the same time, he is growing in his ability to evaluate the content and style of his writing. His goals are becoming more specific, especially in his reading log when he states that he should not begin sentences with *and*. (Note: Jonathan's learning log and writing components are not pictured.)

Reading-log sample

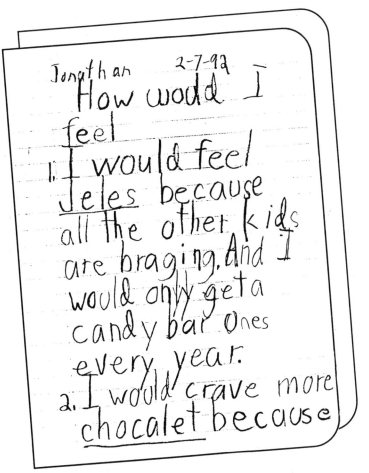

Jonathan 2-7-92

How would I feel

1. I would feel Jeles because all the other kids are braging. And I would only get a candy bar ones every year.

2. I would crave more chocalet because

Vame: Jonathan   Date: 3-23-92
Reading Log
This sample shows that I can write a character trait about Charle. I can put pereods at the end of santen.

goal After a pereand I do not need a And.

Student evaluation

3/26/92
Reading Log
Jonathan, in this reading response you were able to compare your feelings with Charlie's feelings. Your sentences are interesting.

Teacher evaluation

Mid-Quarter Letter from Jonathan Concerning His Writing Goal

At the end of the second quarter, Jonathan stated that his goal was to write more stories "as good as the clown story." To help Jonathan focus on this goal, his teacher suggested he write a letter to her explaining how he was going to reach that goal. In this letter he says he is reaching his goal, because now he is comfortable showing people his stories. One story he is proud of is "Elmer Comes Back."

Mid-quarter letter

> Dear Mrs Laase,
>
> My writing goal is I will keep on writing like my clown story. I am reching my goal. The way I keep track is I can show people. One is Elmer comes Back I like my story.
>
> signed, Jonathan

Selections from Jonathan's Fourth-Quarter Portfolio Components

Jonathan's portfolio partner, Steven, read Jonathan's work samples this quarter and wrote a positive comment for each.

Reading Log

For his final reading-log entry, Jonathan chose a response to a picture he had drawn of his favorite part in *When I Was Young in the Mountains* by Cynthia Rylant (Dutton, 1982). In this evaluation he states that he can write about how a character feels. His portfolio partner noticed that he used commas in a list.

When I was Young in the Mountains

My picture takes place in a lake. Peter is getting baptized. He gets pushed under water and he sees a frog, a fish, and sea weed. It's day time. Every one is watching. He's happy.

Portfolio partner comments

Name Jonathan   Date 6/3/92
Reading Log Sample
My sample shows that I can put periods at the ends of my senenses. I can write how a carkecter feels.

Student evaluation

Name Steven   Date 6/5/92
Portfolio Partner
Jonathan puts coamas in his list. Jonathan made capitals after every sntice. He rote netly. Jonathan icsplans the sory.

Learning Log

Jonathan chose this discussion of the heart to include in his portfolio. His evaluation shows that he is still concerned with mechanics. Steven, his portfolio partner, wrote an evaluation, too. Notice his positive comments.

> Jonathan   May 27, 1992
> Heart
>
> The Heart has two parts. The Hert has two valves on each side. The Heart has veins and arteries the veins carry the blood in the arteries carry the blood. When one valve opens the other closes.

> Learning Log
> Name Jonathan   Date 6/10/92
> I can write about the heart
> I can put periods at the end of my sentenses.
> I can put uper cass letters at the begining of my senteces

Student evaluation

> Name Steven   Date 6/10/92
> Portfolio Partner
> Jonathan exspaned about the hart. He put periods and capitels. He learned abt about the hart.

Portfolio partner comments

Mid-Quarter Letter from Jonathan Concerning His Writing Goal

Jonathan's fourth-quarter writing goal was to write a story by himself and publish it. When asked to reflect on his writing goal, Jonathan realized that he had not yet reached it. He was still writing with others. This prompted Jonathan to work on a story by himself.

> May 15, 1992
> Dear mrs Laase,
> I am not reaching my writing goal I writ with other people. I'll try to reach my goal.
>
> Love,
> Jonathan

Mid-quarter letter

Writing Sample

Jonathan chose a paper he had written about marsupials. He reached his fourth-quarter goal as he researched and wrote this paper by himself. His portfolio partner was impressed with the big words Jonathan used!

> The male red kangaroo goes 30 feet in each hop the size of a school bus. Kangaroo's are called living pogo sticks.

Writing sample

Vame Jonathan   Date. 6/10/92.
          Writing Sample.
I can write about marsupials.
I can evaluat my writing
I can do resurch on a story.

Student evaluation

Portfolio partner comments

NameSteven   Date. 6/10/92
          Portfolio Partner
Jonathan rote big words.
He put periods and capitels
Jonathan lerned alot about
koalas.

ALEXIS'S PORTFOLIO
(UPPER-ELEMENTARY: fifth grade)

Baseline Sample

This learning-log sample was selected the first week of September to use as a baseline. Writing- and reading-journal baseline samples were also included. This is the only time Alexis was not involved in selecting samples for her portfolio.

Student's folder

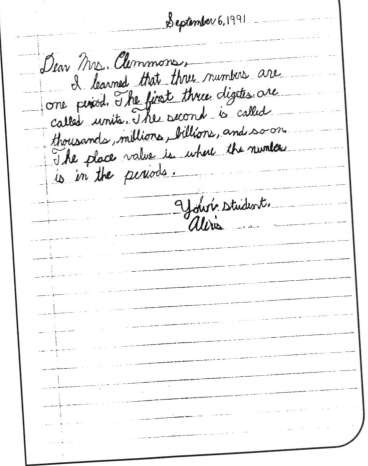

September 6, 1991

Dear Mrs. Clemmons,
    I learned that three numbers are one period. The first three digits are called units. The second is called thousands, millions, billions, and so on. The place value is where the number is in the periods.

          Your student,
          Alexis

Baseline sample

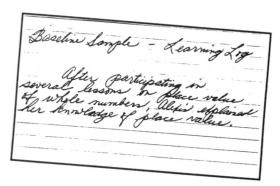

Baseline Sample – Learning Log

    After participating in several lessons on place value of whole numbers, Alexis explained her knowledge of place value.

Explanation of baseline learning-log sample

Selections from Alexis's First-Quarter Portfolio Components

Shown here are three of the five components Alexis included in her portfolio this quarter.

Reading Journal

Alexis's baseline reading-journal sample was a retelling of a book she read. This sample, taken in the first-quarter, already indicates growth. She relates one book she is reading to another she has read and gives her opinion of what she would do if she were the character. After reflecting on her response, Alexis realizes that she wants to explain more about the book she is reading. Her goal is to improve her comparison of books by writing more about the book she is currently reading.

Reading-journal sample

> October 16, 1991
>
> Dear Mrs. Clemmon,
> Besides Mallory on strike I'm reading The Hot and Cold Summer. I think it is good.
> I really love Johanna Hurwitz type of writing. It reminds me of a book I read a long time ago. I forget what it was called. It was about a girl named Lizzy and her friend who went through life together. But when they start sixth grade Lizzy wants to be cool. The book tells about how much Lizzy wants to join the cool croud so she leaves her other friend.
> If I were Lizzy I would not give up my friend just to be cool.
>   Sincerly,
>   Alexis

> 1st Quarter
> Alexis, this reading response shows that you can relate this book to another one that you read. You can give a brief summary of the plot and tell what you would do if you were the character.
>   Mrs. C.

Teacher evaluation

> Alexis   10-23
> This sample shows my parents and teacher that I can compare books, that I have read, and that I am reading. I personalized my response and gave my feelings.
>   Goals:
> My goals are to write in paragraphs. I will write more things about the book such as the plot, the setting, and the characters. In my comparing I should write more about the book I am now reading instead of only telling about a book I've already read before.

Student evaluation

Record of Literature Read

Alexis kept a record of the literature she read and included this list in her portfolio each quarter. In reflecting on her list this quarter, Alexis set a goal to read a greater variety of literature.

Reading record

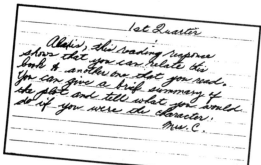

Reading Log

Date	Title, pp	author	Genre	Rating
9-5-1991	Follow my Leader 187	J. Garfield	Fiction	Easey
9-11-1991	Worry Week	A. Lindberg	Fiction	Easey
9-18-1991	Sarks Castle	S. York	Fiction	average
9-21-1991	Three Happy Soldiers	L. Wilder	Fiction	average
10-4-1991	Stacy's Mistake	A. Martin	Fiction	average
10-18-1991	Mallory on Strike	B. Martin	Fiction	average
10-21-1991	Billions of Bats	M. Schlein	Fiction	Easey
10-21-1991	How to think like a	S. ...	Fiction	Easy
10-28-1991	Hot and Cold Sw	J. Hurwitz	Fiction	Easey

Writing Sample

In a writing conference, Alexis concluded that her draft of a story needed more dialogue. As she revised the story, she added more speaker tags and some narration. Alexis notes in her evaluation that she learned to paragraph and punctuate dialogue and to make her story action-packed. She decided on her goal after readers of her story wanted to know more about her characters. In her next story she wants to more carefully develop the main character. The teacher's evaluation reflects strength in composition and style.

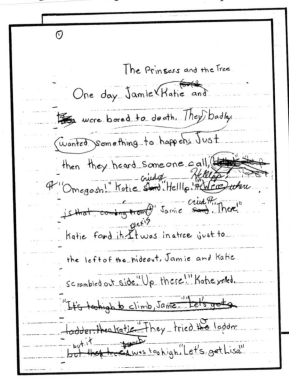

Writing sample (first draft)

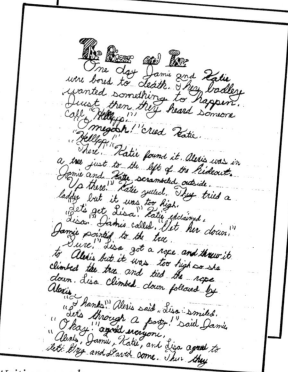

Writing sample

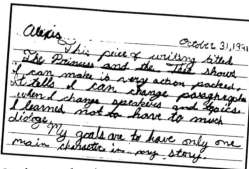

Student evaluation

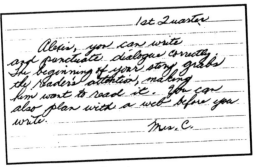

Teacher evaluation

Portfolio Conference

During the portfolio conference, Alexis was invited to share her portfolio with her teacher and to explain how her samples show what she had learned in reading and writing. As Alexis talked, her teacher recorded her comments. The conference concluded with Alexis stating her goals for the next quarter. She then read the goals that her teacher recorded and signed her name, indicating that they were stated accurately.

Student's Name *Alexis*

Record of Portfolio Conference

Date *11/1/91*

Goals

Student's Comments

Teacher's Comments

Enthusiastic writer
Interesting responses
I agree with your evaluations.

You have set excellent goals for yourself.

I know how to write in complete sentences. I write down what I think about the topic. I can listen carefully and read carefully. I can write and read well. I learned in writing a story to not have too much dialogue — that is, not to have dialogue only. I also learned I need to have one main character and have an exciting plot.

I learned to use the Wonder and Wonder chart to help me write reading responses. I learned to use think about strategies in reading. They help me. In reading, I learned to read more than just fiction books. My favorite author is Jean Fritz. I like the way she writes funny books. She makes them humorous and makes you want to read them.

• To write about more than 1 topic in my reading responses.
• To read 35 minutes every night.
• To use the Wonder and Wonder chart more in my reading to help me understand.
• Add action instead of all dialogue to my stories. Have 1 main character.
• Research and study a topic and then write about it. (William Dawes and Molly Pitcher, for example.)

Alexis

Portfolio conference record sheet

Selections from Alexis's Second-Quarter Portfolio Components

In addition to components shown here, Alexis also included a reading journal response, an audiotape of a book talk she gave to a small group of students, and a list of books she read during the quarter.

Learning Log

This learning-log response indicates that Alexis is writing in the content areas and can write for different purposes. She understands various concepts about pendulums and can explain them in writing as she notes in her evaluation. She includes a web to show that she reflected on what she learned and organized her thoughts before writing. Her interesting style of writing—asking a question and then answering it in the paragraph—is noted in the teacher evaluation.

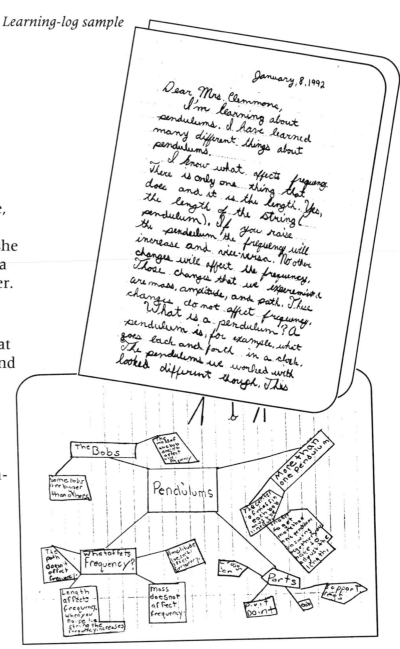

Learning-log sample

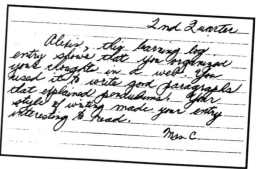

Student evaluation

Teacher evaluation

Writing Samples

Alexis included this story to show that she attained two of her goals: to add action and to have one main character in her stories. It also reflects skills she is learning in mini-lessons: expanding sentences, using descriptive language and vivid verbs, and using a thesaurus. Her reading is also helping her to expand her vocabulary. Alexis wants to continue to improve her story writing and set two more goals for herself: to have more action and to describe the main character better.

Writing sample (first draft)

Writing sample

Student evaluation

Teacher evaluation

Selections from Alexis's Third-Quarter Portfolio Components

Alexis chose these samples for her portfolio plus an audiocassette of a book talk she gave to a small group of students and a list of books that she read during the quarter.

Reading Journal

When she wrote a response to the novel *A Swiftly Tilting Planet* by Madeline L'Engle (Farrar Straus & Giroux, 1978), Alexis related an incident in the story to the Indian Removal Act. In comparing these two events, she shows a higher level thinking that might not be reflected in other types of assessment.

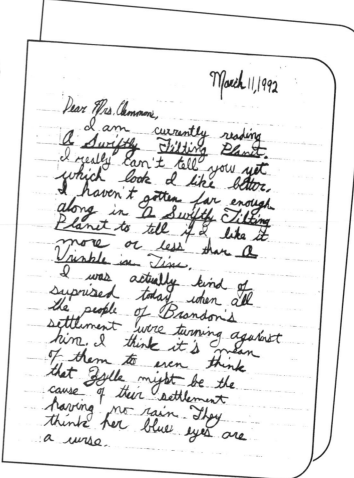

Reading-journal sample

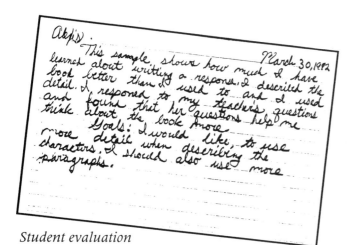

Student evaluation

Teacher evaluation

Learning Log

In this sample, Alexis wrote about her feelings and opinions concerning the Indian Removal Act.

Learning-log sample

> March 10, 1992
>
> Dear Mrs. Clemmons,
>   I feel very sad about the Indian Removal act. Probably, if Jackson hadn't urged Congress to put that act into progress Indians would still be present today. The Indian Removal act was pushed by Jackson because of his hatred of Indians. He had no right to just push out the Indians just because he hated them.
>   When the Indians moved they didn't sign an agreement. They just were baned from everywhere east of the Mississippi. They didn't get to hire an alstate relator to sell their houses and help them look for new ones. Oh no, they

> alexis.   March 31, 1992
>   This sample on the Indian Removal act shows how I feel about it. I learned that Jackson was really the one who led the act. I really think I expressed my feelings well.
>   Goals: Write more about what the topic is than my feelings.

Student evaluation

>   3rd Quarter
>   Alexis, this learning log entry shows that you are thinking about the events you are studying in history. You can express in a very interesting way your feelings and opinions about the Indian Removal Act.
>   Mrs. C.

Teacher evaluation

Writing Samples

This writing sample, a play about Francis Scott Key, shows another kind of writing that Alexis can do. Before writing the play, Alexis researched her topic in several sources and organized the information on a data-retrieval chart (also included in the portfolio). This is a perfect example of how reading and writing are integrated across the curriculum.

Writing sample

> Narrator
>
> Terra Rubra
> Act: 1
> (Key is about 9 years old)
>
> Grandma—When you speak you must let your voice flow. Make people believe you.
>
> Francis Key—Yes grandmother. Thank you, I will.
>
> Grandma—Now, I will send for a carriage to take you home.
>
> (Key climbs into carriage and rides home.)
>
> Francis—Hello, Ann! I'm home!
>
> Ann—Francis, you're finally back! I'll race you to the tree!
>
> Francis—Catch me if you can!
>
> (Race to the tree and tie)
>
> Francis—Terra Rubra is the most beautiful

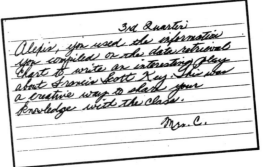

> Alexis   March 31, 1992
> This play shows I can use all of my information and form an interesting way of sharing it. I can gather infor from several sources.
>
> Goals: I need to make things clearer for the listener. I need to express character's feelings.

Student evaluation

> 3rd Quarter
> Alexis, you used the information you compiled on the data retrieval chart to write an interesting play about Francis Scott Key. This was a creative way to share your knowledge with the class.
>   Mrs. C.

Teacher evaluation

Portfolio Conference

During her portfolio conference, Alexis explained how reading helped her become a better writer. She also discussed how writing helped her in reading. Her comments were recorded so that they could be shared with her parents. The written comments also serve as a record of how Alexis views herself as a reader and a writer.

Record of Portfolio Conference

Student's Name _Alexis_

Date _4/2/92_

Teacher's Comments

Student's Comments

Goals

- Exciting to read your writing.
- Much progress in reading and writing.
- I agree with your evaluations.

My reading helps my writing. I use the vivid words I learn in reading in my writing. Sometimes I'd like to write a sequel to a book I'm reading, so I use that idea in my writing. My writing in the reading journal helps me because I can look back on the book. I don't forget what I've read. I don't forget my predictions I write, so I have things to look for in the book. My favorite author is Madeleine L'Engle. She writes about such crazy things. In my writing I use some things that have happened in my life and in my friends' lives. Just like professional writers, I've sometimes come to a place and don't know what to write. I've thrown some stories away and started over. I try to use different ideas. (We discussed the need for planning before writing.) In my fifth grade I've learned to understand books. I've learned so much. I use the charts (Wonder + wonder, Think Aloud strategies) to help me understand. Writing in my reading journal helps me understand. Reading the words is like a puzzle. When

- Write a summary sentence or paragraph at the end of an essay.
- Proofread everything I write.
- Explain at least 6 vivid words each week.
- Read 12 non-fiction books.

Alexis

you summarize, think about the book; it's putting the puzzle together.

Record of portfolio conference

Selections from Alexis's Fourth-Quarter Portfolio Components

Alexis chose a learning-log entry, a reading response, an audiotape of a book talk, a writing sample, and the list of books she read this quarter for inclusion in her portfolio.

Writing Sample

Compare this writing sample to Alexis's baseline and early writing samples to see the great strides she has made in writing. By including her drafts, Alexis also shows the progress she made in writing revisions. In lieu of the teacher evaluation, Amanda, Alexis's portfolio partner, wrote a positive evaluative comment.

Differences Beetween the North and South
One of the very important differences between the north and south was geography. In the south the climate was ~~hot~~ *warm* starting in late March and early April. It started to get cold in late September and early October. That left a long growing season in between for good, money crops such as tobacco and cotton. The soil was rich with few mountains or rocks. However, in the north the soil was rocky with many mountains and hills. It was

Writing sample (second draft)

Differences Between the North and South
By Alexis
One of the very important differences between the north and the south was geography. In the south the climate was warm starting in late March and early April. It started to get cold in late September and early October. That left a long growing season in between for good money crops such as tobacco and cotton. The soil was rich with few mountains or rocks. However, in the north the soil was rocky with many mountains and hills. It was still cold during late March and early April, while the south began growing crops. It got cold earlier in the north, leaving a shorter growing season.

Though the north could grow few crops, the south grew crops for a living. Agriculture in the southern states was important for two reasons: one, growing crops and selling them to the north gave them enough money to make a living, and two, they could grow crops and eat them without using much money. The invention of the cotton gin helped greatly. The north grew some crops like wheat and oats but not money crops like cotton.

Even though agriculture was important to the

Writing sample

Alexis   June 3, 1992
This report shows that I can accomplish my goals. I can paragraph correctly and I know alot about the North and south. I can write in report form.
Goals Write letters to my family over the summer. Finish 3 Stories this summer.

Student evaluation

Amanda 4V. Portfolio Partner   June 10, 1992
This sample shows that you can plan, and use your info well. You can also make your paragraphs and sentences flow together so that piece will be interesting. You can use vivid vocabulary.

Portfolio partner comments

Graph of Books Read

In addition to keeping a list of books that she read, Alexis graphed the number of fiction and nonfiction books that she read each quarter. She was proud that she accomplished her goal of reading 12 non-fiction books.

Graph of books read

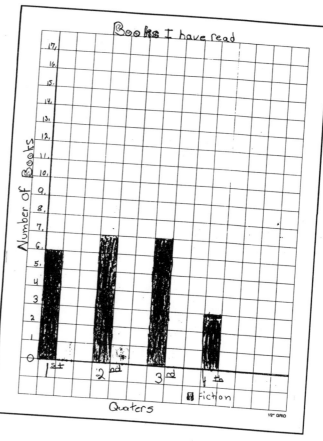

Final Letter

Instead of participating in a portfolio conference at the end of the year, Alexis wrote a letter about how she had grown in reading and writing. The letter became part of her portfolio.

Final letter

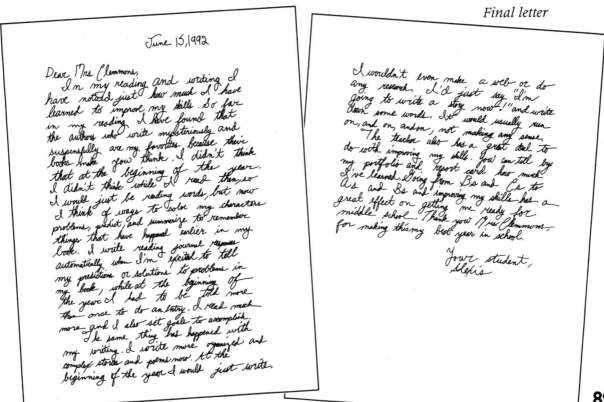

Appendix of Reproducible Letters, Questionnaires, Forms, and Charts

Appendix Contents

📁 News from _____ 📁

This year your child will be keeping a reading and writing portfolio. The portfolio supplements the report card and is a way for parents, students, teachers, and administrators to more easily see a student's progress throughout the year.

Just as professional artists and others showcase their best work in a portfolio, your child will showcase his/her best or most improved samples of reading and writing in literacy portfolios. With teacher guidance, your child will select samples of reading and writing work and add these pieces to the portfolio each quarter. The samples will come from the language arts area, as well as from the content areas: math, science, health, and social studies.

Your child will learn how to evaluate his/her own work and how to set goals for future growth. These evaluations and goals, together with teacher comments, will be attached to each work sample. Your child will bring the portfolio home each quarter with the standard report card.

I am coordinating a parent volunteer program to assist with developing and managing students' portfolios. Volunteers will help organize and assemble the portfolios. Can you please volunteer to help us at school or at home? I will work with interested volunteers on

_____ from _____ in
     (DATE)   (TIME)

_____. I'm looking forward to
     (PLACE)

meeting each of you.

- -

☐ Yes, I'm interested in helping with the portfolio assessment program.

☐ No, I can't help at school, but I can help out at home.

Name _____ **Phone** _____

Child's Name _____ **Teacher** _____

Please return this form to

_____ _____.
     (NAME)   (PLACE)

Dear Parents,

Enclosed is your child's portfolio for this marking period. Please look through the work samples with your child and then send the entire portfolio back to the classroom. The papers stapled together are your child's September baseline samples and the first-quarter samples. The loose papers are samples from this quarter.

Portfolio Contents

1. **Audiotape** (of your child reading a selection of his/her choice and a copy of the page read. The index card includes comments I recorded while I listened.)

2. **Creative-writing sample**

3. **Learning-log sample** (response to a science, social studies, or math concept)

4. **Reading-log sample** (After we discuss how to evaluate a piece of writing and brainstorm the different types of writing we have done, each student chooses a sample of writing to include in his/ her portfolio and writes an evaluation. I also review and evaluate the responses.)

5. **Handwriting sample**

6. **Record of books read** (Children record the titles of books they read each day.)

7. **Questions and responses from the portfolio conference** (This sheet includes the child's responses to questions asked during the conference, as well as the child's goals for reading and writing in the coming quarter.)

Watching your child progress in different areas is so exciting. I hope this portfolio helps capture your child's ongoing development and helps you focus on where to look for improvements in the future. If you have any questions, I will be happy to answer them.

Sincerely,

Dear Parents,

Today your child is bringing home his/her portfolio, reflecting progress in reading and writing. Included are the following items:

The baseline samples are examples of your child's reading and writing work at the beginning of the school year. You can compare later work with these samples to see how your child has grown in reading and writing. Attached to each work sample, you will find my comments, as well as evaluations and goals written by your child. Please examine the portfolio with your child. When you are finished, return the entire portfolio to school.

Thank you.

Sincerely,

Dear Parents,

As you look through your child's portfolio, please take a few minutes to share your thoughts in a letter to your child. You may write your letter on this or any other sheet of paper.

Sincerely,

Reading and Writing Portfolio
First-Quarter Questionnaire

Child's Grade _____   Date _____

We value your feedback on the effectiveness of this literacy portfolio. Please complete this questionnaire and send this sheet back to school. Thank you.

1. What is your opinion of how this literacy portfolio reflects your child's progress?

2. How does this portfolio improve your understanding of your child's progress in school?

3. Which items in your child's portfolio are most helpful to you? Why?

4. In what ways do you think this portfolio supplements your child's report card?

5. Please describe any differences between what the report card tells you and what the portfolio tells you.

 # **Reading and Writing Portfolio**
Second-Quarter Questionnaire

Child's Grade _____ Date _____

We value your feedback on the effectiveness of this literacy portfolio. Please complete this questionnaire and send this sheet back to school. Thank you.

1. As you compare your child's most recent work to the baseline samples (the samples taken from the beginning of the year), what differences do you notice?

2. How does making this comparison help you understand your child's reading and writing development?

3. Do you find the portfolio useful as a supplement to the report card? Why or why not?

 # Reading and Writing Portfolio
Third-Quarter Questionnaire

Child's Grade _____   Date _____

We value your feedback on the effectiveness of this literacy portfolio. Please complete this questionnaire and send this sheet back to school. Thank you.

1. Does this portfolio help you have a better understanding of your child's development in reading and writing? Please explain.

2. Please add any comments or suggestions about the use of portfolios as a measure of your child's growth in reading and writing.

Some Choices for Portfolio Components

1. Reading-journal entries

2. Learning-log entries

3. Writing samples

4. Audiotape recordings

5. Videotape recordings

6. Text samples

7. Records of portfolio conferences

8. Lists of books read

List of Books Read

Name

Date	Books I Have Read	Author	Pages	Type of Literature

Portfolio Conference Questions

Reading

What kinds of books do you like to read?

How do you choose something to read?

What do you do to become a good reader?

What do you do to help remember what you have read?

What goal will you set for yourself to help become a better reader this next quarter?

Writing

Do you like to write? Why?

What are your favorite topics for writing?

Looking at all the papers in your portfolio, what did you learn about your writing?

What goal will you set for yourself to become a better writer next quarter?

Portfolio Conference Evaluation

Name _____ Date _____

Student Comments

Goals   Reading   Writing

Teacher Comments

Guidelines for Portfolio Partner

1. Look closely at your partner's work sample.

2. Write your name and today's date on the top of an index card.

3. Write sentences that answer these questions:

    A. What do you think the sample shows your partner can do?

    B. What do you think your partner did well?

    C. What do you think your partner learned?

Handwriting Evaluation

Writing is something children do every day. They write in their journals. They respond to assignments in their reading and learning logs. They create original stories. Good handwriting is not always a high priority when children are thinking, creating, and writing. As a result, their work does not always look as beautiful as it may sound!

This is a sample of handwriting when writing neatly is the highest priority.

Skill	Comments
☐ well-formed letters	
☐ correct line placement	
☐ good spacing	
☐ no reversals	
☐ capital letters used correctly	

**How to Evaluate Portfolios**

1. Write your name and the date on an index card.

2. Look at your sample.

   A. What does this sample tell that you can do?

   ☞ Think about what you did well in this sample.

   ☞ Think about what you learned.

   B. Write sentences that tell what you can do well.

3. Think about realistic goals.

   A. Skip a line after your evaluation.

   B. Write your goal(s) on your card. Be specific about what you plan to accomplish.

📁 Directions for Audiotape Recordings 📁

1. Clear the counter and begin tape on side A.

2. To record, press both record and play buttons at the same time (or check recorder for other directions).

3. Write the title of the book and the beginning number of the counter on the envelope.

4. Test the machine by saying your name and the date.

5. Rewind and play. If it is loud and clear, continue. If not, repeat step 4.

6. Read from your book for at least 5 minutes.

7. Look at the counter. Write the ending number on the envelope.

8. Rewind the tape to the beginning of the taping session.

9. Listen to the tape with your teacher.

10. After listening, discuss these questions with your teacher:

    ☞ Did I read with expression?
    ☞ Did I correct myself when I made a mistake?
    ☞ What can I say about my reading?

What a Good Writer Can Do: Primary Level

I put periods at the end of sentences.

I put question marks at the end of questions.

I put uppercase letters at the beginning of sentences.

I put uppercase letters on names.

I write the word **I** with an uppercase letter.

I put a vowel in every word.

I leave spaces between words.

I write in complete sentences.

My handwriting is readable.

I can write a friendly letter.

I can write about real things.

I have good beginning sentences.

I have good ending sentences.

I make my characters real.

I reread and revise my writing.

I can write stories with a beginning, a middle, and an end.

I can use describing words.

I use onomatopoeia words.

I can write poetry.

Criteria for Effective Writing: Upper Elementary Level

I can write complete sentences that are not run-on sentences.

I can write a variety of sentence types.

I can write compound sentences that are connected with words like **and**, **or**, and **but**.

I can write a good topic sentence in a paragraph.

I can write supporting sentences to help support the topic sentence in each paragraph.

I can write accurate nonfiction that is interesting.

I can plan before I write.

I can write stories that have a beginning, a middle, and an end.

I can describe the main character well.

I can write a story with a problem and a solution.

I can explain the plot clearly and in order so people can understand what I am writing.

I can stick to the topic of the story.

I can write a story with narration and dialogue.

I can use interesting and vivid words.

I can confer with others when I revise.

I can edit my drafts.

I can use correct punctuation in dialogue.

Writing in My Reading Log: Primary Level

I can tell the main idea of the book in a summary.

I can tell how I thought the character felt.

I can write about a book in a friendly letter.

I can retell the story.

I can describe a character.

I can predict how a story will end.

I can rewrite the story with different characters.

I can write about the traits of a character.

I put periods at the end of sentences.

I put question marks at the end of questions.

I put uppercase letters at the beginning of sentences.

I put uppercase letters at the beginning of names.

I write the word **I** with an uppercase letter.

I put a vowel in every word.

I leave spaces between words.

I write in complete sentences.

My handwriting is readable.

Criteria for Writing Responses to Literature: Upper Elementary Level

I can predict.

I can use vivid words.

I can describe the characters.

I can describe how the characters feel.

I can compare myself to a character.

I can tell who the character reminds me of and why.

I can tell how I would act if I were the character's brother or sister.

I can tell what I would do if I were the main character.

I can discuss the plot.

I can tell about the conflict and how the characters solved it.

I can discuss the theme of the book.

I can compare my own story that I'm writing to the story that I'm reading.

I can describe the setting.

I can tell if the setting is integral or backdrop and why.

I can compare two or more books by the same author.

I can describe the author's style of writing.

I can discuss the author's point of view.

I can discuss the ending of the book and explain how I would change it.

I can give my opinion of the book and tell how I would change it.

 # Writing in My Learning Log: Primary Level

I can write story problems.

I use scientific words.

I can explain how to do something.

I use mathematical words.

I can explain what I learned.

I put periods at the end of sentences.

I put question marks at the end of questions.

I put uppercase letters at the beginning of sentences.

I put uppercase letters at the beginning of names.

I write the word **I** with an uppercase letter.

I put a vowel in every word.

I leave spaces between words.

I write in complete sentences.

My handwriting is readable.

Criteria for Writing in the Learning Log: Upper Elementary Level

I can explain what I learned.

I use interesting vocabulary.

I can explain how to solve problems in math.

I can explain a science experiment.

I can explain what I learn in social studies.

I can use scientific words.

I can use mathematical words.

I can write what I understand.

I write in complete sentences.

I can write paragraphs.

I write about one topic in a paragraph.

I use correct punctuation.

Criteria for Public Speaking
(Videotaping)

I am prepared. When necessary, I research, outline, interview, and practice.

I know my material thoroughly.

I can wait until I have everyone's attention before beginning to speak.

I can motivate my audience.

I can speak to an audience for one of these reasons: to inform, to move to action, to convince, to entertain, or to arouse an emotional response.

I can speak slowly and distinctly.

I can glance at my notes when needed.

I can speak with feeling.

I can speak with a natural voice.

I can use gestures to help express meaning.

I can use facial expressions to express feelings.

Author Profiles

Joan Clemmons is a fifth-grade teacher and a past nominee for teacher of the year from Rolling Valley Elementary School in Fairfax County, Virginia. As a language arts consultant, lecturer, and workshop leader, she has made presentations on integrated language arts and portfolio assessment to a variety of audiences across the country, including the International Reading Association and the National Council of Teachers of English. Mrs. Clemmons is featured in *Making Meaning*, a new video series from the Association for Supervision and Curriculum Development on organizing and assessing integrated language arts. She has been a contributor to *Portfolio News* and a resource to many teachers who have observed in her reading and writing classroom. In addition to teaching fifth grade, she has taught grades three through twelve.

Lois Laase is a teacher at Rolling Valley Elementary School in Fairfax County, Virginia. She also has had classroom experience in several other states, as well as in the International Schools in Norway, Italy, and Brazil. While living in Australia and Brazil she was the Community Liaison Officer at the American Embassy. She has published whole language thematic units and had articles published in educational journals. She has shared her expertise on integrated language arts and portfolio assessment at local and state conferences as well as at both National Council of Teachers of English and International Reading Association conferences. She is listed in *Who's Who in American Education, 1992–93.*

DonnaLynn Cooper has taught elementary education for ten years in Fairfax County Public Schools, Virginia. She received her master's degree in gifted education from the University of Virginia. Mrs. Cooper's experience includes teaching integrated language arts, in-depth research, and hands-on use of portfolios in the classroom. Mrs. Cooper has provided a variety of workshops and presentations on integrated language arts to numerous schools and educational forums at the county, state, and national level. Her professional credits include nomination for Teacher of the Year from Rolling Valley Elementary, selection by Fairfax County to develop integrated language arts curriculum, and author.

Nancy Areglado is a reading specialist at Rolling Valley Elementary School in Fairfax County, Virginia. She is an independent language arts consultant and presents nationally. In the summer months she is a consultant for the Bill Martin Pathways to Literacy conferences. Nancy has taught kindergarten through grade eight and served as an adjunct instructor at North Adams State College in Massachusetts. She has served as a language arts coordinator and as an early-childhood consultant for two Massachusetts school systems. She has a number of articles published in educational journals as well as in *The Whole Language Catalog* by Kenneth Goodman, Lois Bird, and Yetta Goodman